VIA Folios 169

Also by Anna Monardo

The Courtyard of Dreams

Falling In Love with Natassia

After Italy

All rights reserved. Parts of this book may be reprinted only by written permission from the author, and may not be reproduced for publication in book, magazine, or electronic media of any kind, except in quotations for purposes of literary reviews by critics.

© 2024, Anna Monardo

Cover photo provided by the author from a family photo album.

Library of Congress Control Number: 2023952411

Published by
BORDIGHERA PRESS
John D. Calandra Italian American Institute
25 W. 43rd Street, 17th Floor
New York, NY 10036

VIA Folios 169
ISBN 978-1-59954-216-4

AFTER ITALY
A FAMILY MEMOIR OF ARRANGED MARRIAGE

ANNA MONARDO

BORDIGHERA PRESS

Table of Contents

Prologue: The Dress	15
Chapter 1: The Template	22
Chapter 2: The War	33
Chapter 3: *Matrimonio combinato*	46
Chapter 4: Yonkers	54
Chapter 5: A Student of Marriage	57
Chapter 6: Anarchy	67
Chapter 7: Prophetess	75
Chapter 8: The Courtyard	86
Chapter 9: Easter	93
Chapter 10: My Father's Accent	111
Chapter 11: Urgency	116
Chapter 12: A Love of the Road	124
Chapter 13: More Urgency	130
Chapter 14: The Cat	132
Chapter 15: Caesura	144
Chapter 16: The House	149
Chapter 17: Our Red Suitcase	168
Chapter 18: Nonna Catherine	177
Chapter 19: The Basement	183
Chapter 20: The Diary	186
Chapter 21: Joliet	198
Chapter 22: *I fidanzati*	201
Epilogue: Inheritance	205
Afterword by Adriana Trigiani	209
Acknowledgments	211
About the Author	215

To the memory of

Stella Martelli Monardo

They that give up essential liberty
to obtain a little temporary safety
deserve neither liberty nor safety.
—BENJAMIN FRANKLIN

It's a brutal business, making
Americans.
—"This Is Living,"
CHARLES D'AMBROSIO

Duòpu tant'anni, amici,
(du' sièculi tra puòcu)
accettàti sti cuòsi cuòmu sùgnu,
cuòmu v'i dicu
e cuòmu vue i cridìti

After so many years, my friends,
(almost two centuries)
accept these things as they are,
as I tell them to you,
and as you believe them.

—*u Vizzarru,*
FRANCESCO FAZZALARI

This is a work of creative nonfiction based on the author's memories and family documents. Some names and other details have been changed to protect people's privacy. A few scenes and dialogues are composites of actual events and conversations that were combined and/or condensed. Some people portrayed in this memoir may have memories of events that differ from the author's.

Prologue

The Dress

> *Whether tomorrow she would love him, or he her, as much as this, or more, or less, no one could say.*
> —*The Evening of the Holiday*, Shirley Hazzard

I've always known it's bad luck to try on a wedding dress before you're engaged, just as it's unlucky to receive a gift of gladiolus, the funeral flower. These lessons were taught to me by my Calabrian kin. Like the ancients, we use our superstitions and supplications to placate the gods, who have us in their teeth when it comes to the two most bewildering aspects of life: death and marriage.

But there was a Wednesday afternoon in 1990, in my New York apartment, when I stood up from my desk, walked away from the manuscript I was copyediting, and reached into my closet, confident it was now safe for me to lift the blue dry-cleaner bag over my mother's wedding dress. Two nights earlier, sitting on my tall kitchen stool as I made coffee (or was I pouring wine?), my boyfriend of three years—I'll call him Sam—had wrapped his big hands around my waist and said, "Let's get married."

The gown was a graying waterfall of lace and silk that Gramma Stella had sewn for my mother, Catherine, when she married her second cousin, a doctor a decade older than she was. I'd been shocked when I learned, as a kid, that my parents had had an arranged marriage. Growing up in suburban Pittsburgh and the first of our clan born in the U.S., I wanted to believe our family had blossomed from nothing less American than a love match. I didn't like that Mom's parents had picked out the guy, and then brought her back to Vazzano, our Southern Italian village, to meet him.

"If I didn't like him," my mother explained, "I wouldn't have had to marry him. But I liked him right away." And just as reassuring was their wedding album—as large as a coffee table and with the heft of Moses's tablets. There was my mother holding her cascading bouquet, my father in white tie and his serious wire-framed eyeglasses. In the photos, their smiles were so lush, I felt sorry for any family that wasn't us.

As I got older, though, I couldn't help but notice my father's pinched frown as he delivered his daily goodbye kiss somewhere in the vicinity of my mother's face, and then her checked fury as she received not the actual kiss but its shadow. Rarely did I see them touch.

In time, I concluded that a marriage that looked good at the start might be the most dangerous match of all, giving no hint of when the joy would unravel, who would get hurt most, and how. My favorite let's-play-house scenario was *Let's pretend we're divorced.* "We each have a baby," I'd suggest to my playmates, "and we know how to drive." None of the women in my family had a driver's license, which, I concluded, was another source of unhappiness.

I did learn to drive, went to college, had jobs. And now was my chance to slip the lace wedding gown off the cloth-covered hanger. It was a struggle to pull the gown over my shoulders and down my middle. My mother had been an 18-year-old bride who weighed barely one hundred pounds, but I was a 35-year-old bride-to-be. Though smaller in stature than my mother, I was fleshier than a skin-and-bones teenager. Gently, I tugged. I'd been waiting for this moment since I was a kid.

"Come on, Mom, let me see it," I had begged one day when I glimpsed the gown in the cedar closet she was organizing. "I won't try it on, I just want to look."

"If I pull that dress out," my mother told me through gritted teeth, "I'm going to burn it." I was saddened by her disappointment, which I assumed was the price of having agreed to an old-fashioned marriage. I vowed I'd know exactly what I was in for when it finally came time for me to get my hands on that dress.

Except here I was, and in the mirror, I saw clearly this wasn't the wedding dress for me. Even with the zipper gaping open, I couldn't exhale. The forty-year-old lace was close in color to my winter pallor.

I did a half-turn and watched the long train swoosh out to the side, a sweet movement. "Okay," I said out loud, "I got this out of my system." In truth, it was a relief to disqualify that heirloom gown, infused as it was with my parents' murky history.

If you're really doing this, I told myself, *make it new. You and Sam can be happy.*

But as I lifted the skirt to pull the gown up over my head, it got stuck at my shoulders. If I tugged, the fabric would rip: sacrilege. If I pulled the skirt down again, I'd have to wear the dress for the rest of my life.

I'm a prisoner in my mother's wedding dress.

I was fully aware of how, in the retelling, I could play up the comedy of this moment. *Somebody, quick, call the fire department!* But with my head swathed in faded lace and my arms stuck over my head like a person under arrest, I recognized the bad joke I was caught up in and I started to cry.

I heard the strained fabric rip a tiny bit as I worked my way free of Mom's wedding dress until I stood there exposed—a 35-year-old woman unable to imagine for herself a marriage different from what she'd witnessed as a child. I had left home young, rebelled in a thousand ways, but I would never wipe out the bad news about marriage that was written onto my bones.

Sam and I were engaged for about fourteen days. We never officially ended our betrothal: We didn't break up, we just stopped saying *wedding*. His proposal had been sincere, but it's likely he was trying out the words *Let's get married* to see how they'd sit with both of us. We'd been moving toward and away from marriage for a good part of our time together. In fact, the evening he proposed, we'd just returned from a therapy session during which it became clear it was time to decide one way or the other. Sam had tried tipping us toward *Yes*.

All my life, I'd gone around asking friends, "How do you know when you're in love? How do you know who's the right person?" Then I met Sam and didn't have to ask anymore. Sometimes when we worked in different corners of my apartment on a Sunday afternoon—he was a journalist, but he was also, like me, writing a novel—I'd look over at him and, without the ambivalence and with much less fear than I'd felt in previous relationships, I'd think, *Marry me*. Maybe I should have broken with tradition and asked him myself.

When we rode the subway out to his apartment in Brooklyn, I'd glance at him wedged next to me in the crowd, close my eyes, and see our children. I'm just over five feet tall, he was over six feet, and I imagined our daughter with his long legs, his blue eyes, our dark hair, reading her way through all our books. Maybe on her way to the fridge she'd stop at the piano to improvise, just as he did. Maybe wandering the apartment, she'd sing beautifully, just as he did. I could see all of it clearly, including the part where he and I would grow old and cranky and lean on each other as we rode up and down Broadway on the M-104 bus.

Even during our most difficult talks, there'd be that moment when he'd kiss the top of my head and say, "What a fine head," or I'd cup his face in my hands and say, "What a *punim*!"

Why would you leave the person who aroused so much tenderness in you?

A night or two after Sam's proposal, despite our obvious nervousness—tiny arguments were sprouting up between us, and when I was alone I often started to cry—we met Sam's parents in a restaurant, as we did now and then. During our weekends at their country house playing tennis and Scrabble, I'd begun to feel real affection for them. This night we met at a downtown restaurant, in an area unusual for all of us. I'm not sure who picked the restaurant or why. The evening felt slightly off-kilter and turned even more so when, mid-dinner, we told them our news.

Did we all hesitate the slightest moment before the hugs and the request for a bottle of champagne? As soon as it was poured, I went to the ladies' room—down a dark stairway, I remember that—and stared into the mirror over the sink, thinking, *Where is my happiness in this?* My hands tremored, my mouth was dry. Panic.

Come on! You and Sam can do this, and it'll be different. Better!

If only he could have said or done something to reassure me completely and forever. But he brought his own anxiety into the mix. "What if we got married," he'd asked a few times, "and had a baby, and I never finished my novel?"

"Sam, honey, I want you to finish your novel," I told him more than once. "What I want is for us to be married at least a couple of years before we have kids." I was four years older than Sam, and, as my father, an OB-GYN, reminded me frequently, I wasn't getting any younger, but couldn't Sam see that the writing—his and mine—meant as much to me as it did to him? By now, the marriage question had whipped up so much apprehension, we weren't seeing each other clearly. He'd look at me and see a potential trickster; I'd look at him and see a prospective lout.

Early in our relationship, we had a game we played—mostly in bed—of making up stories set in different epochs and on different continents. A dacha in pre-revolution Russia, a port city in Brazil, Trieste during World War II. Each story involved lovers who met, underwent dizzying turmoil, withstood heartbreaking separation, and were miraculously reunited. The lovers' names were always our names. It was always us, coming together despite huge obstacles, living over and over again the joy we had felt when we found each other. One afternoon during our agitated engagement, as Sam and I sat on the beach, I spotted a sailboat offshore and, trying to get us back on track, I began, "See that boat, there's a man out there," but it was forced. We couldn't breathe life into the man, or build his boat, or navigate the sea he traveled in his effort to reunite with his beloved. The details took us nowhere. Our imaginations were no longer engaged with each other.

Fourth of July weekend was when Sam and I broke up—officially. Never in my life had I listened to country music (and never have I since), and I rarely listened to blues, but for the rest of that summer, Kathy Mattea and Bonnie Raitt wailed from my apartment while I did rewrites for my first novel.

One of my long-standing wishes had come true: I was working with a fabulous editor who had accepted my novel. She'd given me a

December deadline for revisions, but the work was like carrying rocks. After the breakup, my apartment felt scoured by a sterility so severe that it seeped into my dreams. In one recurring dream, I was giving birth in a white high-tech delivery room with not one person present to help me, though I kept calling out. In other dreams, I'd find myself in landscapes so destitute, I'd wake up parched.

I craved grass under my feet. I was impatient while riding the metallic elevator that separated my apartment from the outside world. On Sundays, as often as I could, I'd leave the city and visit friends who had moved to Nyack, a small town about thirty miles north and sitting prettily alongside the Hudson River. That kinder setting—waterfront trails, river breezes, sailboats—was so comforting, I eventually sublet my apartment in the city and moved up there.

It worked: In Nyack, I felt soothed. My home was a garden apartment attached to an old stone country house. To reach the mailbox, I walked across a tiny patch of yard. Moving out of the city was a good idea.

But it was also a bad one. Slouched in my plastic lawn chair with my feet in the grass, no longer rushing around the city every day, I had long stretches of time to consider why, at 36, I was sitting alone. *Because you're not bold or brave enough.* Or maybe it was an evil eye thing. Was I cursed? Maybe I had a genetic defect because my parents were second cousins. My mother's maiden name was the same as her husband's, which was not unusual in a town as small as Vazzano, but could that be the problem? Or was it an inherited habit of mind, a peasant's limited worldview? I wished for a series of tasks to perform, as in a fairy tale, so I could finally release myself from the Old World curse.

Years later, I would hear a radio broadcast about epigenetics, the study of heritable changes within genes that do not involve DNA, but, rather, occur when someone experiences trauma so extreme that their body is changed on the cellular level. If they have children, the physical manifestation of the trauma can pass on to the next generation, even to those who never experienced the original damaging events. This science would immediately resonate with me, but I would be tripped up by the word trauma. What specific trauma was there in our family?

Immigration, yes, but everyone had eventually landed well. So, whose trauma? Mom's? Gramma's? Dad's?

Before my breakup with Sam, I had believed that a lifelong "American-style" marriage—joyous alchemy of passion, companionship, and equity—was still possible for me, even though it had been slow in coming. After we finally separated, I felt myself slipping into a kinship with my mother and grandmother that was almost sisterly, as if we were equals, none of us more capable than the others of shaking whatever Old World spell had been cast over our hearts. *You thought you could do better, but no.* It was almost as if I were an emotional "mule," smuggling the dark story of one generation into the next without knowing the value or exact nature of what had been strapped onto me.

Chapter 1

The Template

> *Yet life is not a vision nor a prayer,*
> *But stubborn work; she may not shun her task*
> —"Epochs," Emma Lazarus

"You Monardo women," one of our Pittsburgh cousins said to me once, "you don't have much luck in marriage, do you?" He was talking about my mother, her mother, and me. He liked to provoke, so it was important never to show outrage at anything he said.

"We're not unlucky," I told him. "We're unimaginative. We keep having different versions of the exact same marriage."

To tell my family's story, I could dig in anywhere—1915, 1950, 2024. I could begin in Italy, Pittsburgh, New York, or Nebraska. Begin with my parents, my grandparents, or me, and from every point of entry, our story is the same: three generations unhappy in love.

Let's begin in autumn 1929, in Vazzano, our mountain village. Crossing the piazza is a pretty 14-year-old. Walking toward the communal fountain, she gazes downward, as she's been taught. In the eyes of her townspeople, her *paesani*, she has the appearance of height rather than actual height because she's taller than her mother. In this region where skin tones range from pale to North African dark, her complexion is eggshell white, and if she had to work in the fields, she'd be burned to a crisp. Luckily, her parents were able to apprentice her to a seamstress, which raises the girl—raises the whole family—up a notch on the social ladder, from peasant to *maestranza*, the class of carpenters, cobblers, seamstresses, and other tradespeople.

These days, everyone walks through town carefully, not just timid teenage girls. It's *Anno VII* on the Fascist calendar, seven years after the rise of Mussolini, and the squeeze of the dictatorship is felt throughout the country, even in tiny Vazzano. Villagers openly opposed to the regime or those who simply fail to demonstrate enthusiasm for it are taken from their homes at night and threatened with clubs, are slapped in public, have their businesses closed down. Most Vazzanesi are peasants working the land, though many have immigrated to North and South America, pushed out by generations of poverty and misery. The epicenter of the earthquake of 1783 was just nine miles away from Vazzano, in the city of Vibo Valentia, and the same was true for the earthquake of 1905. There were cataclysms so severe that rivers changed their course. In 1906, Mount Vesuvius erupted. In Messina, a tsunami followed the devastation of the 1908 earthquake. Born into this land of hopelessness, the young girl knows that the most reliable lifeline is the money immigrants send back to Vazzano, though that source would dwindle during the Great Depression.

Electricity did arrive in Vazzano four years ago, and there are now two paved streets. During a downpour, though, the unpaved byways still turn to mud. The girl can't imagine a different life.

After retrieving her family's water at the fountain, she rolls a rag into a cushioning crown on her head and balances the sloshing tin jug as she walks home. Her dark braid is thick and lush, suggesting, for a man who might be looking for it, an inherent sensuousness, but the braid is also primly coiled at the nape of her neck, no stray hairs daring to fly. Clearly, she is *tutta casa e chiesa*—all house and church. A good woman.

She'd never let on that she's nursing a broken heart from a romance gone bad. Nothing more than a few occasions when she locked eyes across the piazza with a boy her age. Maybe he passed a few notes to her when she knelt at Mass with her friends. *Maybe* there was a moment when they actually spoke while she collected water at the fountain. But then the romance suffered some reversal or lapse that could never—in that place, at that time—be talked out between the 14-year-old girl and that boy who looked at her with so much nice attention. She still aches.

And now the girl's mother tells her that a man has asked to marry her. He's older and has just returned from *"Braddicki!"* This Pennsylvania steel town, Braddock, has attracted many Vazzanesi, including this man who has saved a little money and is looking for a wife.

The girl says, "No!" He's nobody she cares about. Her people know his people, of course, but to her he's nobody, a stranger. *No!*

"Marry him," the girl's mother tells her. "He'll take you to America."

The girl knows what *America* means. She still remembers, even though she was only 11 then, the arrival of a car full of new furnishings that Paolo du Terremutu (Paolo, son of The Earthquake) had acquired after his return from six years in the U.S. Now, they say, he's planning to send his oldest son, Alfredo, to Vibo Valentia to study in *scuola media* and eventually to *l'università*. Only America—the money it's possible to make there—could give a man these ideas. Maybe her mother is right about the man from *Braddicki*.

In time, this young girl and the older man, Stella and Giuseppe, will become my grandparents, but they are still basically strangers to each other on their wedding day, December 12, 1929. Although Giuseppe is a month short of 28, on the marriage certificate he's 23. That four-year error in the groom's age—is it a registry mistake or an intentional muddying of the truth? Does the girl's youth, together with the significant age difference between bride and groom, strike someone as slightly not right? For young Stella, this arranged marriage does have the feel of a dream that's moving forward too hastily, and her anxiety will never completely dissipate during the fifty-two years they will be married. A few days before the wedding, Stella's brothers walk the nine miles to Vibo Valentia to purchase her wedding accessories, but they come back with two unmatched, white high-heeled shoes.

Years later, she'll tell me, "That's how we started out. On the wrong foot, for sure."

On October 21, 1930, when Stella is six months shy of 16, she has a baby who is named Caterina, after her paternal grandmother, according to tradition. From the moment of their naming, Vazzano's babies are both blessed with and beholden to an ancestral bond. The first daughter and son are named for their paternal grandparents, the next daughter and son for their maternal grandparents.

In many ways, Giuseppe is a fine husband. Waiting out the Depression, he stays in Vazzano for three years and sets up his family in the little house that was part of Stella's dowry. Then, in late November 1933, just after Caterina's third birthday, he leaves to return to Braddock, the company town for the Edgar Thomson Steel Works, ten miles east of Pittsburgh. As he did before his marriage, Giuseppe works as a laborer in the mill, sending money back regularly, so his girl-wife and their child actually live better than many in Vazzano.

"We had a charge account at the shop," my mother told me. "It was like a general store. I'd take my friends there, and I'd get an ice cream, but those other kids, they were hungry, so they'd ask for a piece of cheese or something to eat. Then I'd tell the guy to put it all on my father's tab." My mother's whole life, even during her early childhood of peasant poverty, she was swaddled in a thin veil of privilege that she counted on.

After Giuseppe left Vazzano, Stella had to wait almost four years, until she was 22, before he had enough money to buy passage to the U.S. for her and Caterina. As she waited, she sewed: Sheets, pillowcases, bedspreads, tablecloths, napkins—all had to be handmade. On looms, she and her friends wove long, heavy panels that they hand-stitched together to make bedspreads wide enough for the nuptial bed; then, according to their abilities, the girls added six or seven inches of decorative crochet to the edges, transforming a piece that was originally coarse into something quite pretty. And in the same way, Stella took the bits she knew of Giuseppe's life in America and embroidered stories to entertain herself and her friends as they worked. He was called *Joe* there; he and his brother Paul were saving for a liquor license so they could open a bar and be independent of bosses.

"The bosses, are they bad in America? Harsh?" the young women wondered. "And the houses, are they big?"

Sewing their dowries, talking and speculating—that was how they waited the long wait to emigrate, to marry, or to find out from their fathers and mothers what would happen to them next.

"Oh, how bad I wanted to leave for America," Gramma told me when I was a kid, "but Joe's letters never said it's time. Years pass, and I'm thinking I'm going to be an old lady and die there for sure. Then one night I dream I'm walking to the cemetery, and on that road are lined up all the Madonnas, one after the other. Madonna del Carmine, di Pompei, del Gesù. All of them, because I loved them all. And I kneeled down in that dream and prayed to every Madonna. And the last one—Madonna del Carmine, I think she was—was holding a letter in her hands. And do you know, a week after that dream—one week!—the letter came from Joe telling me which boat to come to America."

The women in our family have always looked for and honored the signs from above telling us what to do.

Crossing the Atlantic, Stella came down with an illness serious enough that she was admitted to the ship's infirmary, and little Caterina was left in the care of her godmother, Comare M., part of the group of townspeople traveling together. Once a day, her *comare* held Caterina up to the infirmary window, where Stella waited and waved. Retelling the story, Mom always said, "I had to make sure my mother was still alive." Meanwhile, that ship rocked. Wet tablecloths covered the tables so the plates wouldn't slide off. The terrors of that ocean crossing never left her.

My mother was almost 7 years old when she and Gramma Stella arrived in the U.S. in May 1937. By then, though they still worked in the steel mill, Grampa Joe and his brother had opened their tavern. They lived upstairs in an apartment they had readied for Stella and Caterina. The place was cavernous, bigger than Vazzano's main church, with six large rooms and many wide hung-sash windows looking down onto the corner of Eleventh Street and Woodlawn Avenue.

Gramma must have been astonished. The kitchen had not only running water but also a gas stove and oven. The family's toilet was downstairs one flight, but there was indoor plumbing. No shower or tub, but that was true for almost half of Braddock's households at the time. Over on Library Street, in the basement of the Carnegie Library—America's first!—were public baths for the mill workers to use before going upstairs to the billiard rooms, swimming pool, and gym. The library was where Grampa Joe and his brother bathed weekly. Stella and Caterina made do with tubs they filled with pots of hot water, but Stella wasn't hauling pails from the town fountain anymore.

In the kitchen, plunked down in the center of the linoleum floor, were a brand-new wooden table and chairs and a matching Hoosier cabinet. Painted Depression green, a pale shade popular in the 1930s, the dining set was an investment, as well as Joe's exuberant display of welcome for his wife and child.

On Sundays, especially in the early years, the family got dressed up and took the streetcar to Kennywood amusement park to ride the carrousel. Or they'd stroll the avenue or visit the homes of the *paesani*. When my mother talked about her childhood, she described an indulgent father. All her life, she gave him the benefit of any doubt, admitting he was stern, but emphasizing how generous he was.

Though he worked down in the bar day and night, he'd take a minute now and then to come upstairs with a Coca-Cola for Caterina, and, I'm guessing, long looks at Stella, who was strong and voluptuous, with intense, dark eyes. Did it take his breath away to realize his wife was there, finally living in his home? I hope it did.

Joe called his tavern "the beer garden"—as a kid I wondered where the flowers were—but the patrons nicknamed it the "Blood and Bucket" for all the fights that broke out down there. Was it reassuring or unsettling to Stella that Joe kept a baseball bat behind the bar and on occasion had to use it? His customers came in after their shifts and every night of the week except Sunday. That was Joe's one day off, but only because he'd lose his liquor license if he did business on Sundays. He was like the mill, never quit, too afraid business would collapse if he stepped back for even a minute.

Smoke spewed from the furnaces twenty-four hours a day, prompting the town's motto: "What Braddock makes, the rest of the world takes." Men from Poland, Czechoslovakia, Hungary, Ireland, and

Italy—including both my grandfathers—as well as African Americans from the Southern states were hired to work in Carnegie's steel mills. Some found solace and distraction standing at my grandfather's bar, spittoons at their feet.

When Stella and Caterina arrived, Braddock was a town verging on a city, one-and-a-half miles long and a quarter-mile wide. A block up from Grampa's bar was Braddock Avenue, the main thoroughfare. What did Stella and Caterina think as they walked the avenue, passing Bernie Blumenfeld's butcher shop, the Woolworth five-and-dime, the Famous Department Store, Hahn's Furniture, the Stanley photo studio, Och's Dairy, Nill's Bakery? Separate shops for fish, sausage, poultry, cheese, bread, nuts, flowers. The Capitol Theater, the Paramount— movies showed all week!

Marriage had brought Stella to all of this.

From the avenue, brick-paved streets rose up the hills lined with clapboard houses. Tiny yards with shrines to Madonnas and saints. Each ethnic group had its own Catholic church: St. Brendan's and St. Thomas's for the Irish; St. Joseph's for the Germans; St. Michael's for the Slovaks; St. Isidore's for the Lithuanians; and St. Mary of Mount Carmel, the Italian church, where Stella and Caterina went to Mass. There were temples and chapels and storefront churches. Two rival public high schools, plus St. Thomas High School. On opposite corners from each other, two banks.

At St. Thomas School, four months after arriving in the U.S., Caterina began first grade and became Catherine. She learned her new language quickly, as children do. Stella and Catherine often walked to the convent, rang the bell, and waited for someone to answer so they could hand over a warm loaf of Stella's homemade bread. "I loved the nuns," my mother said of her teachers, "but some of them were real doozies." They smacked her left hand to force her to stop writing with it, just one of the sanctioned assaults that convinced my mother she didn't quite measure up, a shadow cast over her confidence that stayed with her all her life. Left-hand-bashing was standard in that era, so surely Catherine saw other kids get the same "correction." Still, it must have been hard not to take it personally when the nuns brought the ruler down on you.

Stella's and Catherine's willingness to meticulously comply with the rules set down by any authority had been hammered in while they still lived in Vazzano, where, in the men's absence, the older women took on the job of overseeing the younger women's comportment. Even before arriving in Braddock, Stella and Catherine were accustomed to living within a tiny hut created by *not allowed*.

What Joe wanted to eat was what Stella cooked. He didn't want her wearing makeup, so she didn't. Mother and daughter were *not allowed* to go out without telling him where, with whom, and for how long. *Not allowed* to spend money without asking first. *Not allowed* to handle the money. His women—including his many nieces—were absolutely forbidden to set foot in his tavern.

At one point, Stella had to take night classes to prepare for her citizenship test. She liked going to school and wanted to continue, but Joe told her no. *Not allowed*. A woman didn't need education, she just had to be *furba*—shrewd enough to get the better end of the deal at the market.

And when Stella wanted to vote—which FDR election was it? Did she try to discuss it with Joe, maybe after the Sunday meal, when he was halfway relaxed? Probably it was a big *no* as soon as she brought it up. Joe was afraid that in the privacy of the voting booth, Stella might vote Democrat, like her brother Jim.

Uncle Jim and Aunt Mamie Martelli and their many kids lived a block away and were in and out of Stella's kitchen all day long and most evenings, too. During those early years in Braddock, with so many *paesani* from Vazzano nearby, the households were fluid, connected, exuding an aura of deep protection. Stella's family and Jim's were especially close, brother Jim and sister Stella devoted to each other. Joe knew that Stella asked the advice of her brother. *No*, Joe decided, it was best to keep Stella out of the voting booth.

Joe laid down the law, but he never enjoyed it. His patriarchal duties were more burden than privilege. After his brother Paul died—too young—all the work was on him. As a bar owner, Joe was diligent, complying with every restriction governing the selling of liquor in Pennsylvania. Meanwhile, he had to be vigilant about governing his wife and daughter, too. He set himself a tough task: maintaining Old

World propriety upstairs while keeping his unfettered patrons happy in the bar. It was a lot.

With his impatient voice, ventriloquism of his own self-loathing, Joe would yell up to the apartment from the bottom of the steps when he needed something—a cup of coffee or a sandwich because he couldn't stop for lunch. Though his "*Stel*-la!" had an Italian accent, it did sound a bit like Marlon Brando's would in *A Streetcar Named Desire*, but Joe's command was less desperate; he knew he had his wife's full attention.

Catherine was 9 or 10 when her world became even smaller. Sore throat. Strep throat. Penicillin was not widely available yet, and the infection spread to her heart. Mitral stenosis. Per the doctors' orders, she was *not allowed* to roller-skate over the brick sidewalks like the other kids anymore. She lay in bed reading until relatives visited, bringing prayer cards, comic books, and embroidered hankies. But when the visits ended, Catherine still had too many empty hours to think about all she was missing.

Stella had hoped she'd have more children, but when she was in her mid-20s, a doctor determined she needed surgery for a gynecological problem. She may have had some form of cancer—my mother never knew for sure. Could the problem have been a result of having given birth at 15?

The doctor made it clear that surgery was necessary, but no one told Stella she would be unable to conceive afterward. If she had known, she wouldn't have gone through with it, so Joe and Mamie, Stella's confidante and translator, didn't tell her until after the operation. She was desolate—still so young, with no chance for another baby, and her only child chronically ill. That surgery, my mother said, "threw her for a loop." Would it have helped Stella if she'd been able to make a fully informed decision? At what point does a child bride stop being treated like a child?

I think of that tiny family—Joe, Stella, Catherine—living in the sprawling apartment over the bar, and I imagine each of them powered by a separate engine of frustrated but insistent yearning, their domestic choreography similar to the wild-shooting kinesis of the pinball machine Joe had installed in the bar, those slapdash attempts—some so close, others piddling and ridiculous—to hit jackpot.

All three were U.S. citizens by now, but a teenage daughter brought the family to a new, possibly treacherous, border crossing: Exactly how much of the "American ways" was Joe going to tolerate in his home? His daughter wore trousers as often as she wore a skirt. She chewed gum, lived and died with her radio shows. At some point, Catherine had acquired a Brownie camera. After she developed a roll of film, she started talking about a career as a newspaper photographer, as if she were Katharine Hepburn. *Sure, you want your daughter happy, but things can go too far.*

And yet, despite her ambitions, how could Catherine venture out? Due to illness, she was absent from school for months. Doctor visits required frequent trips downtown. Riding the streetcar, Catherine peered out at kids her age, whole gangs of them laughing on their way to school. She was left out. Stella, sitting next to her, looked out the same window, thinking, *I have this daughter with a permanent heart disease. She has no brothers or sisters. As long as I'm alive, I can take care of her, but when I'm gone . . .*

By 16 or 17, Catherine knew she'd never catch up with the other girls—not their grades, certainly not their secrets and gossip. When her friends came to visit her in the big bedroom she had all to herself, a few were already talking about their steady boyfriends. Yet, even as confined as her life was, Catherine did have her eye on one boy, and her friends reported, "You-know-who asked about you, Cathy!"

Her mother overheard and warned, "If you father finds out . . . !"

The boy was Slovak, or maybe Irish—either way, Joe wasn't having it. Not even an Italian kid from Braddock was acceptable to him. What Joe knew best about America was what he'd observed from behind his bar, and men like his patrons weren't getting anywhere near his daughter. His Catherine was going to be with an Italian straight from Italy or no one.

Early in 1948, Stella sat down at her green kitchen table and, made bold by her duty to her daughter—the only bond that superseded her deference to her husband—she wrote the letter to her cousin Anna in Vazzano to begin discussion of a possible match for their children. With her pen poised over the tissue-thin paper, Stella rationalized for herself the step she was about to take: *My cousin lost her husband, Paolo du Terremutu, God rest his soul. Her oldest, Alfredo, is a doctor now, but still, they have all those kids to worry about, and I know since the war, things aren't good over there. Maybe... Maybe...*

As I picture Stella addressing her letter, dropping it into the mailbox, thereby initiating the negotiations that led to my parents' marriage, I can't help but think of Delmore Schwartz's short story "In Dreams Begin Responsibilities"—that scene in which the narrator imagines himself in a theater watching his parents' engagement as if it were a movie, and when it comes to the moment of his father's proposal and his mother's acceptance, the narrator jumps out of his seat in the dark theater, shouting, "Don't do it! It's not too late to change your minds, both of you. Nothing good will come of it, only remorse, hatred, scandal, and two children whose characters are monstrous." My brother and I are not monstrous (at least I can say with certainty that he is not). And, thank God, our family is, in general, too restrained to behave in a way that inspires scandal. But the remorse, the wish to backtrack—that is in our story, just as it is in Schwartz's. And if I push myself toward honesty, I'd have to admit there were moments—extended moments—that could be labeled "hatred."

I had no doubt I could invent a better way to be married.
What hubris.

Chapter 2

The War

> *Life is short, art is long, the occasion fleeting, the attempt risky and the judgment difficult.*
> —Hippocrates quote written on a file card in my father's desk

In spring 2009, fifteen years after our father's death, my brother and I were emptying Dad's desk in Florida—he and Mom had retired there—and we found a faded manila envelope stuffed with five autobiographical narratives our father had hand-written, titled "My Father," "My Mother," "My Father's Family," "Life in Our Village," and "Education." From the simplicity of his language and the focus on historical details, I guessed Dad had written these pages for my brother's two oldest children, the only grandkids born while our father was alive. By then he was 72 and had had various medical complications serious enough to force him to retire earlier than he'd expected.

The day my brother and I found our father's stories, the work was dusty and tedious, so I welcomed an excuse to sit on the yellow shag carpet and read. I was just taking a break. I didn't expect to find the story that explained why our father married our mother.

> *The line between rich and poor was very thin. The rich were also poor.*
> —my father, writing about his village

Alfredo was the firstborn of seven, born in 1920 in Vazzano, in the province of Vibo Valentia. In his stories, he described our village this way:

> There was one paved piazza. The fountain there was beautifully made of steel and covered with branches from four trees, one in each corner. The physicians lived in the big house in the piazza. In another big house on the top of the town had lived the De Sanctis family, the noble family of Vazzano, during the 1800s. By the time I was born, that house was divided into several units, and we lived in one of them. Later on, my father bought another unit that was connected to ours, and in this way he made the largest unit in the building.

Though I've edited a bit, this excerpt and those that follow are true to my father's vocabulary, sentence formation, and voice. I hear his intelligence and love for his village, as well as his unapologetic familial pride. Mostly, though, I hear his voice delivering history lessons to his grandchildren.

> Most of the other houses in town were built with stones or mud blocks or bricks, and were two stories high. The family lived on the top floor. The ground floor was divided, half as stable for the donkey, pig, chickens; and in the other half they stored grains, oil, cheese, beans, and other provisions. When necessary, extra beds were improvised down there for some of the children.
>
> Vazzano's population, less than 2,000, was made up of 80% or so peasants working the fields for larger landowners. There were four or five carpenters; three brothers were the bricklayers; four tailors who hand-made our suits; four shoemakers hand-made our shoes; three general stores; and three *cantine* (bars), where men would meet evenings to play cards, have a drink, talk about politics.
>
> We had one priest and two churches.
>
> Most of the peasants' children worked on the farms or helped the shepherds tend sheep. The children of the tradespeople went to school, and in the afternoon the boys went to their apprenticeship to learn a trade. The girls would go to a seamstress. Children of both sides married within their caste.

Alfredo's journey beyond his "caste"—from peasant, leaping

over *maestranza* and jumping all the way to the "aristocracy" of the professional class—was accomplished by his hard work and perseverance; however, it was his father, my nonno Paolo du Terremuto, who'd had the idea that class-jumping was possible and best achieved through education. Paolo's father was nicknamed "u Terremuto," or "The Earthquake," because of his fiery temperament, but Paolo himself exuded the quiet authority that could make things happen.

Still, the townspeople chided Paolo, "Why would you make your sons better than you?" The Vazzanesi were peasants descended from peasants, and ingrained in them was a grudging, mute obeisance to the nobles who owned all the property and had governed the peasants' labor, economy, and justice system for longer than anyone could remember. From pre-Christian times, one invader after another—the Greeks, Romans, Byzantines, Lombards, Muslims, Normans, Hohenstaufen, Spanish, French, Austrians, the Spanish again, the French again—had colonized and dominated Southern Italy and Sicily.

Eventually, in 1861, with Italian Unification, the southern mainland and Sicily were gathered into the Kingdom of Italy under the first Italian king, Victor Emmanuel II, *Padre della patria*, Father of the Fatherland. And though Italy was now unified, the South was still divided into large agricultural estates owned by barons who kept the peasants trapped in quasi-servitude. In the North, tradesmen formed guilds for mutual governance and aid, but in the South, the common man knew only the vertical hierarchy of the patriarchal latifondo system: Laborers were in competition for the landowner's favor, which kept them too disempowered to unify and overturn the status quo. Then, as now, the hoarding of power degraded everyone. In the public sphere, patriarchal rule diminished the male peasant in the same way that women were kept under thumb at home; there, the man could demand obedience, at times with the same physical force the landowner used freely on him.

How could the peasant even attempt revolt against his overlord? The barons' dominance, it was believed, had been conferred by rulers who had received their mandate directly from God. The poet Francesco Fazzalari, a contemporary of my father's and a pharmacist in Vazzano, wrote, "Poor Calabrians, / who think a king is the same as a saint."

This feudalistic mindset was what truly governed the laborer. When it was prudent, the peasant swore his allegiance to every god tiered above him—landowner, priest, physician—but he never surrendered his distrust, which was his sole power and best protection.

> *There has never been since New York was founded so low and ignorant a class among immigrants who poured in here as the Southern Italians who have been crowding our docks during the past year.*
> —an 1882 editorial in *The New York Times*

In 1913, my grandfather Paolo, aged 21, sailed to America with his father. For two years, they worked in the Braddock steel mill, and then they sailed back to Italy so Paolo could fight in World War I. "Assigned to the heavy field artillery," my father wrote, "he reached the rank of corporal major."

Ambitious and determined, Paolo returned to the U.S. after the war, leaving behind his pregnant wife and 1-year-old Alfredo. It was 1921, the same year the Emergency Quota Act restricted annual immigration from any country to 3 percent of the number of residents from that country who were listed on the 1910 census. By design, the law favored Northern European immigrants while limiting the number of Italians and other Southern Europeans, who were considered racially and morally inferior. But Paolo gained entry.

"Instead of working in the steel mill," my father wrote, "he went into business, did very well, and in 1926, he felt economically secure and returned for good to his much loved family and country and town." In the eyes of 6-year-old Alfredo, his father was made larger than life by his years abroad.

> My father's arrival [in Vazzano] I do remember. I was in the midst of a lot of people crowded around a car [taxi] stopped at a point where it could go no farther because the street was too narrow. In that confusion of my father's arrival, I did not see him. Was I shy? However, while the car was being unloaded I tried to keep all the other kids away from "my father's car." When the car left, we kids ran after it, piling up on the back rack. Most of us

jumped off at the corner of the little church, while the most adventurous kids didn't jump off until outside of town. I vaguely remember a big man raising me in the air. And that is what I remember of the "Big Encounter."

Alfredo's account of his father's legendary arrival echoes what my grandmother Stella remembered of that day. Neither of them ever forgot the air of abundance—and possibility—that surrounded Paolo du Terremutu. He had returned home with enough savings to buy land, which eventually became a profitable farm—olive trees to make oil, sheep rented out for fertilization, and hired laborers to help him while his sons went to school. Paolo du Terremutu was still a *contadino*, a farmer, but now the land he worked was his and the profit was his. Some of his earnings were earmarked for his children's education and some, as my father wrote, went to benefit their town:

> To stimulate the economy of Vazzano, my father organized an orchestra, hired a director who taught the peasants and artisans how to play all the instruments. It was exciting to see these young people go to neighboring towns to give their concerts during the religious feasts. Besides the money they made, they felt great, having learned to read not only Italian but also the music.

Not long after the "Big Encounter," Alfredo's father announced to the little boy, who was not among "the more adventurous kids" and who was possibly "shy": "You will become a doctor." It was both a compliment—*I see that you are intelligent enough to go to the university and study the most venerated discipline*—and a command: *You will do this, and you will not fail.*

When he was young, Alfredo was very skinny—not unlike Catherine in her childhood—and plagued by colds, and so the village women made him wear a string of garlic around his neck to protect him from the evil eye. Not the *evil* evil eye transmitted by envy, but a more complex evil eye that could be inflicted upon a child by someone who simply loved him too much, which was what the village women thought Alfredo's father, with his ambitious notions imported from America, was doing to his son.

And yet, Paolo's revolutionary vision for Alfredo's future *was* a form of love, part of what made the father exceptional in the eyes of his son, part of what eventually drove Alfredo's decision to immigrate to the U.S.

Once or twice I asked my father what Nonno Paolo did when he was in America, and Dad told me, "I really don't know for sure."

During a visit in Italy, I asked one of my uncles, who reprimanded me: "Why do you ask these questions? My father was a good man and *basta*. That's all you need to know."

The next time I visited Braddock, I talked to cousins of my parents' generation, who told me that the *paesani* had handed down a story—unsubstantiated and as alluring as a rumor: "They say your grandfather was a confidence man."

"What's that?" I asked.

"One of those con men. They'd get those Italians right off the boat to trust them and give them their money to keep safe—none of them trusted the bank—and they'd take off with it."

Nonno Paolo?

The con man story was never confirmed—or disproved—but it helped me understand why my uncle had stonewalled my inquiry. He and his siblings had lived through such a complicated segment of history that they needed a hero to believe in, nothing less than a saint. Another uncle told me about a time during the Depression when Nonno Paolo got the idea to plant fruit trees along the road that bordered Vazzano so travelers could reach up and grab something to eat, suggesting that Nonno Paolo had a wide swath of humanitarian civic concern in him.

Now, almost a century later, I'm a grateful beneficiary of all my grandfather put in motion; yet I wish I knew the man in his full complexity. I'll never stop wrestling with the question of what, exactly, is my debt to the past.

> *Italy wants peace and quiet, work and calm. I will give these things with love if possible and with force if necessary.*
> —Benito Mussolini

By 1926, the year Nonno Paolo returned to Italy, Mussolini had declared himself Italy's leader: All political parties but the Fascist regime were banned, and the press was largely censored. In tiny Vazzano, Nonno Paolo, an outspoken anti-Fascist, was embattled. A town chronicle recorded that my grandfather was among those "most targeted" because he was "suspected of spreading subversive propaganda." When Fascist rallies were scheduled for the town, he was arrested and held in prison for fear he might cause disruptions.

To attend school, children were required to become card-carrying members of the Fascist youth organization, signing a vow to "follow without discussion the orders of Il Duce and to serve with all my force and if necessary with my blood the cause of the Fascist revolution." Still, my grandfather maintained both his resistance to the regime and his campaign to educate his children.

> When the *cancelliere* (retired town secretary) died, the town gave a big funeral and all the schoolchildren had to participate. Of course, for this funeral the male children would wear the black shirt, their Fascist uniform. My father prohibited me to wear anything black for the funeral because the *cancelliere* and the Fascists had been fighting my father. That morning, I was sent back and forth several times, but my father was IMMOVABLE and would not let me wear black. Finally, he kept me home.

Fellini-esque, this scenario of Alfredo as a little boy running back and forth between his schoolmaster and his father, but the fact is that Alfredo was very young when he began parsing out his allegiance between his father and the Fascists, two powers in direct opposition to each other, two powers that expected much of him.

For middle school and high school, Alfredo had to leave home and board with a family in the city, Vibo Valentia. It was a full day's journey by foot from Vazzano, and yet his father's reputation preceded him. "Because of my father's antifascist attitude," my father wrote, "I had some problems in [high] school, but I succeeded all the time to prove that I was a good Fascist." In order to attend medical school in Naples—still the guiding vision for both father and son—Alfredo not only had to maintain a show of allegiance to the state his father abhorred, but he was also conscripted into the Italian army.

> When WWII exploded, Mussolini wanted medical students to go into military service to continue their studies and serve the country by working in military medical units. I volunteered so my brother would be exempted from the draft—he would certainly have been drafted for the infantry. Mussolini still helped families with six or more minor children, and only one was to be drafted. So I thought it was less dangerous for me than for my brother.
>
> In Naples we were placed in a school building . . . but most of us bribed some officer in charge (gave our salary) and he "ignored" our absence in the evening. Groups of three to four of us rented a room nearby where we studied and slept. However, most nights we spent in underground tunnels protecting ourselves from English air bombing. The Americans usually bombed us in the afternoon.

My father never told us a lot of war stories. He either wasn't able to or didn't think we'd understand, but there was one story he told about a night when he and a friend went to a dance hall. Music, a crowd. Eventually Alfredo and his friend were on opposite ends of the hall, and on the side where his friend was dancing, a bomb dropped and the friend died.

"Oh, Dad, what did you do?"

"What *could* I do? I thanked God I was alive."

It wasn't until I was grieving my father's death, trying in any way possible to keep him present in my life, that I began to read about his war. One book was *Naples '44*, a memoir of the Allied occupation of Naples, written by Norman Lewis, a British Intelligence Corps field security officer. Years earlier, I'd given the book to my father, who'd leafed through it and put it aside. Now, picking up the book myself, I understood why Dad hadn't been interested. Early on, Lewis mentions "that anthill of humanity, the city of Naples itself," and I was offended by the dismissive and ridiculing tone that I see too often used to describe Southern Italy. Farther in, though, Lewis's clear-eyed account of Naples's deprivations and horrors got my attention, as did his unsentimental compassion for what he had witnessed. I couldn't stop reading.

Lewis was telling me the stories my father never did: hunger so extreme that the tanks at the aquarium were emptied because any kind of fish was good for a stew. Butchers carved up their merchandise in such a way that customers couldn't tell if they were purchasing skinned rabbit or skinned cat. Women and children by the hundreds picked through roadside fields to harvest edible weeds. My uncle had once told me that "the worst time was after Christmas, from January until March, when the grass started to grow again," which I assumed meant that spring's milder weather was a reprieve—after reading Lewis's book, I understood that things got better after March because people could eat the new grass and weeds.

When the Allies arrived in September 1943, their hefty military supplies were a stark contrast to the civilians' deprivation. In exchange for tins of food, Lewis reports, housewives lined up on chairs in an abandoned building, offering themselves to soldiers. One haunting story was about a father who sent Lewis a formal letter, politely offering his attractive daughter if only the girl could receive one good meal a day—"[She] has no mother, and she hasn't eaten for days. Being out of work, I can't feed my family," the father wrote. An astonishing number of Neapolitan women—on their own or with their relatives as procurers—turned to prostitution to feed their families.

I tried to imagine the moment when each woman realized, *I'm going to have to do this*. And then I began to understand how much I would never understand about Southern Italy and my father's wartime.

Beyond the "near famine conditions in the city," Lewis described in his war memoir the Neapolitans coping with everything from malaria, typhus, and typhoid to vendettas, the Camorra (Neapolitan

Mafia), and the incessant petty thievery of people who had nothing. The Allies' supplies of medicine were so stripped, penicillin could be found only on the black market.

And then there was the bombing. Lewis writes: "Apocalyptic scenes as people clawed about in the ruins, some of them howling like dogs, in the hopeless attempt to rescue those trapped under the masonry."

> During the war, I was lucky. When Italy and Germany were being defeated in Africa, I was in Bari and my name was drawn to go to Africa. I informed my family and tried to tell them I considered myself lucky to be able to go to Africa to defend my country. However, within 48 hours, my father came to Bari, talked to the major general in command of the Southern Italian Front, and I was assigned at a local hospital a few miles away from Bari. The ship I was supposed to go on to Africa was torpedoed and SUNK about one day before reaching North Africa.

Nonno Paolo, all-powerful father that he was, literally saved his son's life. How alarmed Nonno must have been to read Alfredo's wish "to defend my country." I myself was unsettled to realize that young Alfredo's allegiance may actually have been swayed by the gray-green uniform he'd been forced to wear and by Il Duce's frenzied nationalism. Dad was among the troops assigned for transport to Rome to stand in Piazza Venezia and chant *DU-ce! DU-ce!* while Mussolini proclaimed from his balcony. During one rally, due to the extreme heat and, possibly, his unresolvable ambivalence, Alfredo actually fainted. What kind of psychological gymnastics did my father, as a young man, have to perform to sustain his "good Fascist" public act while remaining loyal to his anti-Fascist father? Maybe he was using politics to push back against his father, as every son must at some point. When a young person claims they feel lucky to defend their country, how much is patriotism, how much is strutting, how much is cowering, and how much is simply resignation?

I can never know who my father was when he was 20 or 21, can never fathom Italy at his time, the limited choices or the convoluted compromises he and many others had to make to survive. One thing is clear: Whatever clash there may have been within young Alfredo between what he believed and what he professed, his unmalleable allegiance was to his father and his vision that education was a peasant's best way out from under autocratic rule. I once asked him, "Did you become a doctor because you wanted to or because your father wanted you to?"

"Both," he said.

Alfredo passed his final exams on July 21, 1945, two years after the Allies landed in Sicily, and almost two years after Italy changed sides and declared war on Germany. Three months after the deaths of Mussolini and Hitler, two months after VE-Day, and less than three weeks before the U.S. attacks on Hiroshima and Nagasaki.

He was now a doctor. Before the war, in discussion with his father, Alfredo had considered venturing to Rome to practice medicine there, but funding and connections would have been needed to launch such a career, and in the postwar devastation, his only option was to return home. His first jobs were as substitute for the *medico condotto*, the town doctor, in villages near Vazzano. A modest start. But then in October, at the time of the olive harvest, Nonno Paolo became seriously ill, and on August 6, 1946, he died. The town's band played Verdi's *Requiem* during the procession to the cemetery.

> So there I was without a job, six siblings and a mother in need. We sold the farm animals, I found temporary jobs. Finally I went to three neighboring towns as *medico condotto*. I had a salary, and there was a bus. And in this way we made some money or at least some food for staples (type of barter), so my brothers could continue their studies.
>
> We planned to send my sister to school with the Sisters of San Domenico. And in so doing, we tried to carry on even this wish of my father, who wanted ALL his children well educated. But our sister and our mother could not be separated, and so she returned home after a few weeks . . . Without my father's encouragement and guidance, [the youngest brother] also quit school. My two sisters left school after the fourth elementary class in order not to leave my mother alone.

This was Alfredo's life when my two grandmothers began writing letters to each other to explore the possibility of a marriage between Stella's daughter and Anna's son. Alfredo's sadness is palpable here, but the profundity of the emotional loss that preceded his decision to marry and emigrate becomes clear to me in his description of a trip he and his father took to Catanzaro, the regional capital, when Alfredo was a child:

> What I remember of this trip is a beautiful dreamy golden opera house. We were seated close to the front of the orchestra, and on the stage I saw soldiers dressed in golden and silver military uniforms, fighting with enormous swords.
>
> Next, I woke up in my father's arms while he was carrying me up the large stairs in the hotel, and I saw myself with my chin resting on his shoulder, and his back in a huge mirror covering the whole wall.

With the "dreamy" opera house and orchestra, the uniformed soldiers ready for any battle, a hotel in a big city, and that image of himself safe with his father, a "big man" who had been to America and back, the two of them captured in an oversize mirror on their way upstairs to bed, it's all there: father as protector, ever reliable, guide into the wider world. In time, father and son would not always align perfectly, just as my father and I didn't always agree, but I am deeply moved to read in my father's stories that at age 72 and fatherless for more than forty-five years, he returned to a moment "in my father's arms."

During the war years, Alfredo had a girlfriend. She was the granddaughter of a family that included the Fascist mayor and several physicians who had undermined a business plan Nonno Paolo had initiated years earlier. Politically and personally, the families were not on good terms, but now that Alfredo was a physician, the powerful clan wanted him for their granddaughter. I have no idea how the woman felt; those who told me the story didn't mention much about her. Alfredo, they said, was largely indifferent to the plan.

And yet, at one point, one of the girl's relatives was being chased by the Allies—supposedly he'd been involved in the accidental killing of a partisan—and Alfredo was the one who risked bringing food to the man while he hid in the countryside, which suggests that Alfredo did care—about the girl, or her family, or his townsman—or why put himself at risk? There are so many contradictions of loyalty in my father's story. There's only one question that anyone still alive could answer with any degree of certainty: "Why didn't Alfredo and that girl marry?"

"Your nonna didn't want that marriage," my aunt told me in a hushed voice that indicated we were close to something true. "She wanted your mother for Alfredo."

Nonna Anna, a woman of serious demeanor, was loving in a different way than Gramma Stella was. When I was a teenager, every time we hugged goodbye, Nonna Anna whispered into my ear, "Do your duty to your parents, *cara*. Get married. It's your duty." I could imagine her whispering a similar call to duty into Alfredo's ear. In that time, in that place, the highest form of family love was personal sacrifice. His life so far hadn't been easy, but he'd always known his path because he knew his role—just move toward the vision, which even after Nonno Paolo's death still hung brilliantly before them: a medical career for Alfredo, to pave the way for all the others to get advanced degrees. But how could the siblings study if there wasn't enough to eat?

The americana. She'll take you to America. That's the one you should marry.

Chapter 3

Matrimonio combinato

> *This generation will not pass away till all these things have been accomplished.*
> —Matt. 24:34

I can't contemplate my parents' first meeting without thinking of Elizabeth Spencer's 1960 novella, *The Light in the Piazza*, in which a wealthy American woman is traveling in Florence with her teenage daughter, Clara, whose perfect beauty masks the tragedy of her injured intellect: Due to an accident, Clara has the mental capabilities of a 10-year-old. Mother and daughter are befriended—pursued, really—by a handsome young Florentine shopkeeper, and the mother begins to see an opportunity for her daughter, a path into a future—marriage, children, a sheltering family life—that she had feared wouldn't be possible for the girl. But now, the absence of a shared language between the Americans and the Italian hides the reality of Clara's condition; the girl's playful silliness can be chalked up to an inability to speak Italian. Italy—with its indulgent forgiveness of U.S. tourists, a forgiveness that is really the Italians' native opportunism playing with the touring Americans' guilelessness and lust for romance—is the perfect place to pull off such a trick. And if you're fooling yourself as well as others, is it really so bad? At the novel's end, anticipating her husband's outrage when he learns that his daughter has indeed married the unknowing Italian, the mother says, "I did the right thing. I know I did."

In the aftermath of the wedding that tied Catherine and Alfredo, the chronically ill American girl and the overburdened Italian doctor, I imagine Gramma Stella saying the same thing to herself. *I did the right thing. I know I did.* Repeating it a lot, but never fully believing it.

*

Catherine was 18 when she and her parents arrived in Vazzano on Christmas Eve of 1948. They were no longer townspeople who'd left to find better prospects; now they were *gli americani*, well-dressed travelers loaded down with suitcases, bearers of packaged American foods—crackers, cereal—and warm clothes to distribute throughout the village. In those postwar years, Calabria was dismal, impoverished, brutal in a way Catherine had never experienced. "I was used to radiator heat," she told me, "but all they had was that big tin pot filled with coals in the middle of the room. I was freezing all the time." Gramma Stella, though, was thrilled. During the war years, postal censorship meant she couldn't even send letters to her parents. How grateful she was that they were still alive. And grateful, too, that Catherine's health had withstood the ten-day transatlantic trip, the train ride from Naples, the drive through the countryside, the long trudge back home.

Catherine and Alfredo met the night she arrived. He was a young man with a good smile who made a strong first impression. Quick-witted, picking up on whatever was going on in the room, he had the verbal finesse to smooth out the first awkward moments of any social gathering. That Christmas was only the third without his father. The brothers had taken off their black armbands and the little sisters were no longer wearing black dresses, but the family was still reeling. Alfredo would have covered up that unhappiness. On January 3, ten days after she met him, Catherine wrote in her diary, "Very happy for I love him & want him near," but what did she really know of Alfredo's circumstances? And what did he know about her?

Their mothers—each blinded by love for her child—never considered the possibility of a mismatch. *Who wouldn't want my daughter? Who wouldn't want my son?* But how did they overlook the obvious, which was that in terms of maturity, life experience, and temperament, Alfredo and Catherine were not well suited? A 28-year-old doctor who had served in Mussolini's army and an 18-year-old American girl so homebound by illness and her father's strict rule that her wartime hardships had been blackout window shades and the shortage of silk stockings. They could barely speak to each other.

Alfredo had studied Greek and Latin but knew no English. Catherine spoke unaccented English, could giggle her way through Pig Latin with her cousins, and managed a scratchy version of Vazzano's dialect, but she did not know proper Italian. When did Alfredo realize that Catherine, despite all her advantages, was not as well educated as he was?

Stella was only five years older than her future son-in-law. She'd known him as a kid, but when he was 12, he had gone away to study, and then she emigrated. She didn't know Alfredo personally, but he was from a family she'd always trusted. Because he was now head of *this* family, she had full confidence in him.

Stella herself had had an arranged marriage, *un matrimonio combinato*. The adjective *combinato* takes its root from the verb *combinare*, which means to combine or arrange. *Combinare* can have a negative connotation; for example, *Cosa stai combinando?* means What are you up to? *Hanno combinato qualche cosa* means They've made a deal that's not completely up front. So, *matrimonio combinato* is a wedding with a hint of an ulterior motive to it. Stella understood the exchange: Her Catherine would acquire a doctor-husband to look after her when her parents were gone, and Alfredo would immigrate to the U.S. with all its opportunities and could more easily help his family.

But how could Stella be aware of all that was involved in Alfredo's pledge to fulfill his father's wish, *the education of all the children*? And if Stella didn't know, how could Catherine have had even an inkling?

The house where Catherine's intended lived with his family was smaller than the apartment above the bar, but there were eight of them packed in. Sure, he was a doctor, but there was nothing fancy about him. And yet, even after a short time in Vazzano, Catherine began to decipher the social ladder. The young doctor's home, though spare, had a separate room for his medical studio, and compared with her grandparents' house, his had more windows, more balconies, and a higher-up view, indicating that his family had more clout than hers. She hadn't anticipated feeling intimidated in this backward old town. As an *americana*, she had status and advantages to spare, didn't she?

*

Alfredo could not deny she was pretty. And her mother was a dressmaker, so the whole family was particularly well dressed. The girl not only possessed the brass ring of American citizenship, she was also the only child in a family prosperous enough to leave home for six months. Did Alfredo ever wonder why her parents weren't marrying her off in the U.S.?

Before Catherine's arrival, she and Alfredo had exchanged a few letters and photos. Now, in person, as soon as it was clear the couple were amenable, the real courtship began, following the conventions, which were courtly and full of fluff, camouflaging the uncomfortable reality that two strangers were entering into the most intimate of unions. It was all played out in public. One week while Alfredo was working out of town, his brothers brought Catherine a bowl of fresh cream from the farm, and etched into the surface was a heart and the couple's initials.

There were serenades. At night, Alfredo and a few friends stood under Catherine's grandparents' windows and played guitars and violins and sang. Along with the standard Calabrian folk songs, they probably also belted out bits of opera, because Alfredo loved opera. In the end, it didn't matter which songs they chose: They did it because it was what *fidanzati* did in that place, at that time, but Catherine didn't know the drill. As she—chaperoned by her mother—rushed out onto the tiny balcony, how was Catherine to know that the performance wasn't uniquely inspired by Alfredo's love for *her*? In Braddock, when had she ever heard of serenades? Any singing below her bedroom window would have been a drunken patron crawling out of the bar late at night. In Vazzano, though, the serenade was standard.

Catherine had been steeped in Hollywood movies, so she knew to expect her groom to come bearing gifts (think Frank Sinatra and Ava Gardner, Humphrey Bogart and Lauren Bacall, Clark Gable and Joan Crawford). But she had no clue to the origins of that tradition, in which the groom gave gifts not to express his affection but to display his material goods to the community, to gain status. In earlier times, a groom had to *show* his bride's family that he was capable of caring for her. And the ring? It was to celebrate a successful negotiation between two tribal families.

In Southern Italy in 1949, the transactional nature of marriage was not this blatant, though it was there, imbedded in the rituals, and young Catherine made the mistake (an understandable one, given how naive she was) of believing her arranged marriage was a love match.

To confuse things further, young Alfredo was not courting her with a cold heart. In their engagement photos, Catherine and Alfredo actually gaze at each other. Even with all the calculation at work, even though the union was, first of all, pragmatic, an undeniable delight had bloomed between the couple.

These were Catherine's days of high romance, no less magnificent for being lived against a backdrop of postwar deprivation. Vazanno was a conglomeration of rocks, each stucco or mud-block house leaning on its neighbor, the hard edges scraping the townspeople's worn-thin coat sleeves in their daily passage along the tight, narrow streets.

But in spring, when my parents were formally engaged, the village and all its sharp corners softened. The trees flowered. The streets pulsed with the scent of thyme, oregano, orange flowers, wild roses, and pears. For Easter, Alfredo gave Catherine a Perugina Easter egg wrapped gleefully in bright foil and tied with elaborate, floppy ribbons. The chocolate was dark and delicious, and within the hollow egg, she found a gift—a small brass bell topped with two interlocking circles. I have that bell still. When I was growing up, we used it at the bedside if someone was sick and might need to summon help during the night. That bell survives because it meant so much to 18-year-old Catherine, as did every detail—each hand-delivered note, every picnic and pressed flower—of her whirlwind courtship in Italy.

She fell for it, all that Old World business, and, later in her life, my mother would have a hard time forgiving herself for this. *Mom, at 18, I would have fallen for it, too.* Was no one wise enough to pull her aside to explain how superficial these courtship gestures were? No one was alert to the ways she could be hurt? *Mom, you'd been taught to rely completely on family, and, through my eyes, it looks like they failed you.*

*

One week after Easter, on April 23, 1949, Catherine and Alfredo married in a civil ceremony in Vazzano's town hall. Catherine wore a pink suit tailored by her mother, stood before a public official, and exchanged vows with Alfredo in a language she barely understood. She always referred to this civil ceremony as "our pretend wedding." How much of what happened during those months in Italy, in Alfredo's world, seemed to her to be *pretend*? There was no priest or wedding dress for this ceremony, not yet: She was holding out for her *real* wedding back in Braddock. Alfredo's mother, brothers, and sisters would not be present for that. The only thing Alfredo needed in front of his family was the civil ceremony. If he and the *americana* were legally married, he could enter the States, establish his medical career, and fulfill his duty to start sending money back to his family or resettling some of his brothers in the U.S.—whatever it took for all the siblings to get university degrees and, in time, be reunited.

In June, the newlyweds went on a "pretend honeymoon" with Grampa Joe, Gramma Stella, and even Uncle Jim, Stella's brother. To surprise Stella and their parents, Jim had sailed over using his gambling winnings. What a dream! All of them together.

The honeymoon travelers' primary destination was Naples, to process paperwork for Alfredo's passport. After that business was accomplished, they went on to Ischia, Rome, Florence, and Venice, where they posed for some of my favorite family photos. My father with his arm lightly around my mother's shoulders as they stand within the encircling pillars of Piazza San Pietro. In Piazza San Marco, my mother, hand outstretched offering breadcrumbs and laughing within a rush of pigeons.

Just like Clara in *The Light in the Piazza*, Catherine is dressed beautifully. She really is a lovely young woman. Her dark hair is pinned up in some photos, in others it's curly, loose. Her shoes and purses are coordinated with her outfits. Gramma Stella, 34 years old and mother of the bride, is dressed in refined dark tones and high heels. In every photo, the men are in suit and tie. Borsalino hats. Overall, it was a classier time than now. Sure, they were tourists, but in none of the photos do you see sacks or bags. No one is wearing ugly, comfortable shoes or standing around swilling from a bottle of soda. As a child, I studied these photos of the adults I knew so well, absorbing them in their most perfect incarnation as they stood against the monuments of Europe. I could see little difference between my loved ones in these "honeymoon" moments and the movie stars captured in the pages of *Life* magazine. Princess Grace, Audrey Hepburn—they had nothing on the women in my family. My parents' marriage—my family's whole story—was as good as any movie star's, only better, because it was ours.

On June 11, the bride and her parents boarded the *Vulcania* in Naples to return to the U.S. "Today at three o'clock," Catherine wrote in her diary, "after standing in the port joking with Alfredo, I had to go aboard & we sailed at five o'clock. Alfredo & I throwing kisses to each other. Here I left my love & an ache in my heart began. I wrote to him at night." It was sad to leave Italy and her "pretend" husband, but Catherine and her mother had to get home to start making dresses for the "real" wedding back in Braddock.

Princess Elizabeth (future Queen Elizabeth II) had married Prince Philip in 1947, and that royal wedding was Catherine's model as she planned her own church ceremony. Elizabeth had had a fifteen-foot train attached to her gown; Catherine had a fifteen-foot veil. The queen had had eight bridesmaids and no groomsmen; Catherine had ten bridesmaids. The no-groomsmen worked well for Catherine, because she had a lot of girl cousins, and if they partnered up to walk down the aisle, she could include them all.

Also, conveniently, Alfredo didn't have any guy friends who needed to be included. They did find him a best man—a doctor or lawyer from Italy, an educated immigrant that someone knew and everyone agreed would be appropriate to stand with Alfredo as he waited at the altar.

*

Alfredo arrived in the U.S. on November 27, 1949. Immediately, with his rudimentary English, he began contacting the Pittsburgh hospitals for work; in the evening, he took English-language classes. I wonder how long it was before he became aware of the noun–verb errors and double negatives that were common usage in Braddock: *He don't have a car, she ain't coming to the show, they don't know no better.* None of that was present in my mother's speech by the time I knew her, but as a child of Braddock, she must have absorbed and used some of those phrases.

I can imagine him correcting her (as, years later, he'd correct my Italian). Was this one of the ways she began to feel self-conscious around him, judged and found *not right, not enough*?

Alfredo was a diligent student but he had a lot to learn, and he had to do it quickly. In the two months after his arrival, Catherine was busy, too, with all the details for their church wedding, scheduled for Tuesday, February 21.

"Why Tuesday?" I asked my mother when I was old enough to realize that Tuesday was an unusual day for a Catholic wedding Mass.

"Because it was Shrove Tuesday," she explained. "The next day would be Ash Wednesday, and once Lent starts, you can't have a wedding for forty days, till Easter's over."

Still, why not wait until after Easter and have a regular Saturday wedding like everyone else? That Tuesday-morning wedding always made me suspect that from the start, things were off. Like when Gramma Stella had to get married wearing mismatched shoes.

Chapter 4

Yonkers

> *You have the sense to see you were caught in a story, and the sense to see that you could change it to another one.*
> —"The Story of the Eldest Princess,"
> A.S. Byatt

Who knows how Catherine's parents had described Braddock to Alfredo, but he was shocked by how dirty the town was when he arrived. All day long, umpteen times, Stella wiped down the windowsills, but steel-mill dirt settled there and everywhere else. Before he arrived, did Alfredo know he'd be living above a tavern? He'd survived wartime Naples, so he wasn't delicate, but the rumble downstairs, especially on Saturday nights, was disappointing. He had anticipated a different America.

It was cold, so a more serious overcoat was needed. There was snow. He needed snow boots.

Alfredo's worst shock came when he found no entrée into the medical profession in Pittsburgh. He had graduated from the University of Naples with *110 e lode*—highest grades, highest honors—but in 1950, just a few years after the end of WWII, the hospitals and established medical practices did not welcome a young physician with an Italian medical degree. His father-in-law tried to help, as he'd promised he would, taking Alfredo around town, introducing him to all the doctors he knew—with Catherine's illness, the family had made the acquaintance of several physicians—but Joe was unable to make things happen. Rationally, Alfredo understood he couldn't expect a bartender to promote his medical career, but when faced with his father-in-law's ineffectiveness, he probably felt all over again the deep stab of how much he'd lost when he lost his powerful father. As a young man who came of age in wartime Italy, Alfredo was primed to embrace the anyone-can-become-anything version of the American dream. But he hadn't yet unlearned the habit of patriarchal dependence that was, along with suspicion, a Calabrian's best tool for survival.

And maybe, unconsciously, Alfredo was even a little annoyed with his father, his miraculous father: *You, Papa! You and your America—talking "America!" all the time, making me want to come here and see for myself, and now what? There's nothing here for me. I'm married to this girl who's so fragile she can't leave her parents, and my own family is across an ocean and who knows when I'll see them again, and how am I ever going to learn to understand these people here when they talk?*

Ultimately, the Italian network did save him. Alfredo's brother in Italy had a friend whose brother was a doctor in Yonkers Hospital, in New York. The job offer came by mail: *Report for your internship on March 30, 1950.*

March 30 was the reason for that pre-Lent Tuesday wedding.

But *intern*? In Italy, Alfredo had been a full-fledged doctor. Still, he couldn't be picky after job-hunting for months. He was offered a low salary and student housing. Clearly, Catherine couldn't go with him. Alfredo had no choice but to leave Braddock—and his wife—and go to New York.

Alfredo's departure one month after their wedding was the Continental Divide in the couple's hopeful love. Though they were married for forty-four years, until Alfredo's death, they never fully recovered from the rift that went by the code word "Yonkers." The separation was sad and difficult, not only because the newlyweds had to part but also because by then they were barely speaking, and Catherine didn't fully understand why.

Yonkers was the first stop in my father's American journey. After fifteen months there, he spent the next several years at hospitals in Washington, DC; the Bronx; Santa Cruz, California; and finally the University of Chicago, where he did his residency in obstetrics-gynecology. His solo odyssey stretched out for five years. If my parents ever mentioned the time they lived apart, they referred to it as an inconvenient separation necessitated by my mother's poor health and my father's minuscule income as he established his career in the U.S. Occasionally, at dinner, he'd tell amusing stories about working in ambulances in DC ("If we were hungry and there was traffic, the driver turned on the siren"), and he'd rhapsodize about the beauty of coastal California ("reminded me of Calabria!"). But because he downplayed the details and my mother was equally close-lipped, and since it all happened before my brother and I were born, this part of my parents' story seemed to me ancient history—part fairy tale, part myth, fully irrelevant. For all I knew, every marriage included a tedious separation.

My mother was reunited with my father in the summer of 1955, in Joliet, Illinois, where he had joined an OB-GYN practice. The following April, I was born. After five years separated, my parents resumed their life together. The way they told the story, their reunion was as seamless as if the separation had never happened.

Chapter 5

A Student of Marriage

Who wants to compute the speed of history?
Like all falling bodies, it constantly accelerates.
—*Angle of Repose*, Wallace Stegner

"I'm glad I wasn't born in Italy," I said to Gramma Stella when I was 5.

"How come, dear?"

"Because every lady born in Italy doesn't like her husband."

"Oh, dear, that's not true! I love your grampa. Mommy loves your daddy."

Gramma never raised her voice at me, but I knew from her pinched-together eyebrows that I'd said something "not nice."

And yet, I wasn't convinced I was wrong. Eavesdropping, I'd follow Gramma with her extra-long telephone cord in and out of the rooms of her rambling apartment as she cleaned, sewed, or kneaded bread while confiding with one or another of her *comare*. I heard her voice rise in complaint: "That *disgraziato*, you know what he said to me?" Or go soft with compassion: "He did that to you *again? Cretino!*" It was clear that she and her friends had to work hard to manage the difficulties their husbands brought on. My earliest notion of marriage was that for women, it was a full-time, worrisome job. *Don't let Grampa see that. Don't make Grampa mad!*

For six months when I was 3, my parents and I lived with my grandparents in the apartment above the bar. Dad had just left the U.S. Army, and we'd returned from two years in Paris, where he had been a major stationed at the American Hospital. While in France, we were able to drive to Vazzano for summer holidays—a dream come true for Dad. Eight years had passed since he'd seen his family.

In winter, his youngest sister lived with us. She was 20 years old and my favorite playmate. For Mom, she was as dear as a younger sister. While we lived in Europe, my parents' two worlds melded. Though Catherine missed her parents horribly, this was a golden time in her marriage. Together, Mom and Dad took a trip to Amsterdam and another to Switzerland while their friends in Paris took care of me.

When we returned to the U.S. and civilian life, we moved in with my grandparents. Dad was arranging to open his first private practice. Mom was pregnant with my brother, Paul. On Saturday nights, I'd lie on my belly on the living-room floor to peer through the heat vent down into Grampa's bar. The jukebox played, and I glimpsed smiling women dancing with laughing men. Happy noises filtered up. "Gramma, let's go downstairs!"

No! Not nice!

Gramma and Mom never went near the bar, because Grampa said so. Why did the wife have to be nervous around the husband? He was never nervous around her. Impatient, sometimes bossy, but not afraid. How come only the wife had to be scared?

There was a sort of joke Grampa occasionally repeated that concerned Gramma's hair, which had never been cut. In the morning when she loosened her plait, her black hair fell down the length of her back. Pulling the full mane over her shoulder, she'd comb and braid, then pin her braid into a crown around the back of her head. There was no denying her hair was lovely. But if Grampa heard someone compliment Gramma, his line was, "Yeah, lots of hair, no brains."

"Grampa, that's not nice."

"He's just kidding," Gramma said.

"But, Gramma, it's not funny. You're really smart."

"That's enough," she warned me.

The only problem at my grandparents' was that there weren't other kids around to play with; other than that, I would have been happy to live above the bar and spend my days with Gramma forever. I liked to kneel on her rocking chair at the kitchen window and look down at the mechanics working in the garage across the street. Behind the garage were the train tracks, and then, way beyond, towering, the slow-moving Ferris wheel at Kennywood park.

Next to Gramma's kitchen was the storage room, where the cousins hung their homemade *soppressata* to dry—the cool, dark *cantina* offered the best conditions for the sausages to cure. Two windows opened onto an air shaft and let in little light. The dim *cantina* was filled with shadows, so I huddled close to Gramma when I followed her in there. I was eye to eye with the steamer trunks she and Mom had brought with them from Italy when Mom was a little girl. Occasionally Gramma opened one of the trunks, and it exuded a strong, stagnant scent that I imagined was the captured air of Vazzano. At Gramma's, we were in two places at once.

One evening while we lived in Braddock, snow was deep on the avenue, and my father lifted me onto his shoulders and walked me through the crowds moving in every direction. I was at such a great height, I could almost touch the streetlamps and holiday lights, and I could feel—actually *feel*—how very happy Dad was as we strode down to Woolworth's. This was a night or two after my brother was born.

When I was almost 4 and Paul was one month old, we moved to a rented house in Swissvale, then two years later to a house built just for us in Forest Hills, a suburb not far from Braddock. There was a fireplace and two bathrooms with bathtubs, another bathroom with a shower, and a powder room: four toilets! We had a laundry chute that sent our dirty clothes down to the basement. A turquoise dishwasher. And, for the first time, I had my own bedroom. For several nights, I was so dazzled by my canopy bed, I had trouble falling asleep.

On one of my first evenings at the new house, a girl came by as I played in our driveway and said her name was Joy. I said, "But *joy* means happy, so that can't be your name." But she explained that Joy could also be a name, and I believed her, because she was tall and starting second grade in September. She was a year ahead of me, but Joy became my first best friend.

In many fascinating ways, Joy was different from me. She really was tall, and her straight, blondish hair was side-parted and obeyed her barrette, which kept her hair out of her eyes. She resembled the girls illustrated in my new reading book. My hair was long and frizzy. I wished I had American hair that was smooth and didn't have to be dealt with daily by my mother. "Ow, you're hurting!" We stood at the powder-room sink while Mom worked a dampened comb through my tangles. Joy waited in our hallway so we could walk together to school.

She was the only child of quiet and kind parents, and they lived in one of the first purely American homes I spent time in. Their living room had books stacked on the floor, and the parents sat together and read in big chairs near the fireplace, where now and then we'd pop popcorn in a corn-popper. I tried to describe this long-handled basket to my mother, but she kept buying Jiffy Pop.

At Joy's house, the TV was in a small room where we rarely sat. Mostly we played upstairs in the office adjacent to her father's bedroom. Our games were inspired by Sherlock Holmes and other detective stories that Joy and her parents read. I supplied what I could from the Bobbsey Twins. We never played in her mother's bedroom.

"Her mom and dad really have separate bedrooms?" my mother asked me as she and Gramma made Sunday dinner.

"Yeah," I said. "Her mom's room's all pretty, and his is serious."

Gramma said, "That's not good, a husband and wife in different rooms," and my mother agreed. I was puzzled about why this small detail of bedtime arrangements was significant. My parents, though they slept in the same room and same bed, never sat around together the way Joy's parents did. But why *were* Joy's parents in separate bedrooms? When I asked Joy, she said her dad snored, so I decided the bedroom arrangement was just another reason their house was serene.

Then the worst happened: Joy's dad was transferred to Ohio. I hated the word *transfer* and hated the state of Ohio. After Joy and her parents moved away, an older couple moved into their house. My mother thought they were strange because after dinner they sat on lawn chairs in their front yard and the wife read to the husband—*out loud!* My mother roared with laughter. "As if he doesn't know how to read!" I don't think Mom meant to ridicule the neighbors, she just needed to shake off her unease. The domestic idyll of a couple content in each other's company was not only unthinkable to her but also unattainable.

Another conundrum I encountered in my study of marriage involved the couple next door. They, too, seemed to *want* to spend time together. They had a brick barbecue pit on their patio, where they spent long summer days tanning and smoking cigarettes. They talked a lot together and laughed. The husband was usually shirtless, the wife in shorts and a bandeau bathing-suit top even though she was "no spring chicken."

"Mom, why don't you wear a two-piece suit?"

"Me, with my scar? Give me a break."

So maybe it was Mom's heart condition that disqualified her from being happier. Her scar was from her first open-heart surgery, and it ran down her back, under her left arm and up onto her chest. I tried not to look at that train track that puckered up her skin. I hated when her illness spilled into our days. Some mornings she had chest pain, other days she did not, but I worried all the time, and it was worse when she tried to comfort me. Crying, choking on her words, she said, "If something happens to me, *somebody* will take care of you."

Somebody?

Meanwhile, next door, the pop-music radio station played constantly. Ray Charles's "I Can't Stop Loving You." Bobby Vinton's "Roses Are Red (My Love)." I liked the way marriage looked over there—so much joking around! Our glamorous sun-bathing neighbors had no children, but they were thrilled with their Chihuahuas. My mother had made clear to me that companionship in marriage was strange, and public affection even stranger, but secretly I told myself, "When I get married, it's going to be fun: reading out loud to each other, or lying on a couple of chaise lounges to relax."

Chaise lounge was an American phrase I'd picked up from Joy.

If only they'd had penicillin when Mom was sick. That thought tormented me when I was a kid. If penicillin had been in use during the late 1930s, my mother's childhood strep throat would likely not have developed into heart disease. I would have grown up with a mother who could walk up flights of stairs, ride a bike with me, go on walks. Who knows—she might have been able to learn how to drive. But in the autumn of my second-grade year, Mom went into the hospital with heart failure. It seemed to me she was gone for months, but it was probably a couple of weeks. Gramma Stella moved in to take care of Paul and me. After she tucked me in, made the sign of the cross on my forehead, and left the room, I'd hide my face in my pillow and begin my negotiations with God. *Please, if someone has to die, let it be me.* I couldn't imagine my existence without my mother.

In time, my prayers worked. Miracle granted: Mom came home. At first she spent a lot of time on the couch, and we had to be careful not to hug her too hard.

I'd always known she was enveloped in an ongoing illness, so even before her hospitalization, I had a hard time leaving for school. After her hospital stay, each day's departure became a trial. I walked to the top of our street, pivoted, returned home. *I have to make sure she's okay.* By the time I reached the front porch, I was breathing hard.

"What are you doing back here?" Mom scolded. "Go! You'll be late."

Sometimes it took three tries before I made it over the hill. The snow was deep during our southwestern Pennsylvania winters, and my parents urged me to bring my lunch to school, but that was impossible. I couldn't get through a whole day of second grade without checking on my mother.

Then, one day in third grade, I had no choice. There was a luncheon for the hospital guild Mom volunteered with, and, as an officer of the guild, she couldn't miss it. I had to stay at school for lunch. For some reason, the lunchroom wasn't available that day, so the "lunch kids" had to eat in the second-grade classroom. As I sat at that smaller desk, in that room where I no longer belonged, my sense of displacement was profound. Though I knew everyone around me, I talked to no one, curled into myself as if I'd arrived at a school on a distant continent. I ate what I could swallow, gathered myself, made it through the afternoon. When I got home, my mother hugged me and said I'd done well, and I told her, "I'll bring my lunch again tomorrow."

Even as I said it, I wasn't sure if I was punishing her or me.

"But you don't need to stay tomorrow. I'll be home for lunch."

"But I want to stay at school." And the rest of that winter and into spring, I carried my Barbie lunch box. I became a girl who said goodbye to her mom and walked away and stayed away until school was out, and then maybe even lingered. I'm sure she praised me for being "a big girl," and some part of me probably was proud. My need for my mother was still there; it just went mute and got stuffed away, as if the fraught way I had loved her was an old souvenir—something important but useless, like the mementos tucked into Gramma's steamer trunks from far-away Vazzano.

Every Sunday, my grandparents came to our house for dinner, but during the spring of fourth grade, more than once I heard my parents arguing in their room. Suddenly Gramma and Grampa were no longer "allowed" to visit. That's what Mom said Dad had decided. *Not allowed.*

A few nights when my father was at the hospital late, my mother came to my bedroom and woke me. Crying, she asked, "What would you say if a lawyer asked you whether you wanted to live with Mommy or Daddy?" This happened a couple times. Finally I asked, "Who would take care of Dad?" After that, she stopped waking me.

One Friday afternoon in April, our cousin's car was waiting in the driveway when we got home from school. Earlier that day, after Dad had left for a weeklong conference in Chicago, Mom had packed our suitcases, and now she, my brother, and I were headed "down Braddock," as the usage went. Even at a young age, I understood that no matter how much affection I felt for Mom's hometown, it was a social tier below our neighborhood, where every house had an attached garage and you never had to put a folding chair out front to save your parking space.

Even though Mom tried to pass off our week at my grandparents' as a little vacation, I knew we were in descent. In our whole elementary school, there were maybe three kids who had divorced parents. This thing happening in our family was unthinkable. Worse, no one would talk about it. All week, my brother and I had to share the big bed in our mother's childhood room, and we argued every night about who kicked the most. Going to and from school in a taxi mortified me. Friends asked why we weren't walking. *Aren't you living at your house?*

After dinner, Gramma took us to the drugstore on the avenue for ice cream, but I wasn't interested.

And then on Thursday evening, one of the cousins came to babysit Paul and me. Listening when I shouldn't have been, I'd learned that my mother and grandparents were going to another cousin's house, and Dad would be there. Together, everyone would decide what should happen next in our family. Who was downstairs keeping the bar open? It was rare for Grampa to leave his post, but that night he did.

How many hours were they gone? I tried to get Paul to play Chinese jump rope, but he wouldn't. Nothing good on TV. Finally my grandparents returned with Mom *and Dad*, all of them speaking nicely to one another. Dad carried our suitcases out to his Buick, and the four of us went home. The following Sunday, Gramma and Grampa were back at our house for dinner, and I played the theme song from *Romeo and Juliet* on the piano for them because it was one of their favorites.

And that summer, Mom, Dad, Paul, and I went on a monumental vacation: a Pan Am flight across the ocean, and then stops in Lisbon, Madrid, Paris, Rome, Florence, Venice, and Pisa, followed by a few weeks with our family in Calabria. Until that visit, I'd been aware of my relatives in Italy in the same way I was aware of the silver dollars stored for me in the safe-deposit box at the bank—a valuable but unseen asset I would tap into at some indefinite point in the future. But when the four of us got off the train at Vibo Marina, we entered a gold mine of family. There was Nonna Anna, three of my father's brothers, one of his sisters, and their families (a fourth brother and another sister now lived in Canada). Two uncles were married to two sisters, another uncle was engaged to the third sister, and these couples made marriage look particularly companionable. My brother and I were folded into a group of seven cousins that included three Annas and three Paolos, all of us named after our grandparents. There was one more Anna in Canada, and another not yet born.

Years later, in my first, semi-autobiographical novel, *The Courtyard of Dreams*, the main character, Giulia, is an American girl who, like me, has an Italian father. He sends her to Italy one summer to get to know her family, and she goes grudgingly—she's an unhappy teen. Eventually, though, while at the beach with her relatives, she has a moment of great joy when she looks around and realizes that "everywhere I looked, I saw my family." When I wrote that line, I was in my 30s, but it was a summation of the wonder I'd felt that August in Italy when I was 10.

And when our vacation ended, I was introduced to the fracture within me that I'd feel every time I had to leave my family and Italy. That first summer, we attended my uncle and aunt's wedding in the Santuario di San Francesco di Paola, all the cousins gathered on the altar with the bride and groom. I was a close-up witness to the event, which struck me as so riveting and beautiful, it set the standard for what a wedding should be—set in a marble chapel, spoken in Italian, attended by a jostling crowd, our tangible net of family love. Carried over from that summer and threaded through all my adult relationships was the wish—vague and unformed, but potent—for romance to somehow reunite me with Italy, which was to say, with my family there, and with the highly particular closeness I felt when I was with them. (Such a privately wrought vision, how could an American man know that was in my heart?)

One night that summer as we strolled with our *zii* and cousins to the café for ice cream, my parents were walking ahead of me, and I saw my mother take my father's arm. My aunt whispered to me, "Look! See your parents?"

So, I hadn't been wrong. Something had been amiss in our home. But now, in Italy, everything had been corrected. Our season of unhappiness was over.

Back home, I found that Gramma had left a surprise in my underwear drawer: two training bras and a note—DON'T ADVERTISE THESE. To me, this initiation was proof that our trip abroad had, indeed, remade the universe. Just in time for my transformation into a grown woman, my parents had linked arms and made marriage a happy business again.

Except, as time passed, the mood between them turned grudging, as it had been before our trip. Would Mom move us down Braddock again? One day, I asked her, "When you took us to stay at Gramma and Grampa's, why'd you do that? What happened?"

"Don't put your nose where it doesn't belong," she told me.

A few years later, I went to her again: "Tell me what happened that time."

"How many times do I have to say it?" Her voice was the sound of a gate clicking shut. "The more you stir it up, the worse it smells. Forget it."

Chapter 6

Anarchy

> *"Are you a poet?"*
> *"Maybe."*
> —*Just Kids*, Patti Smith

Mom was turning 40 and Dad 50, and though the times warned *Don't trust anyone over 30*, my parents' parties, always suburban-proper, did gesture toward hip. My parents' choreography as a couple was never smoother than when they were hosting. They loved their many friends, and in social gatherings, the magic happened: The two of them became a third entity that was better than either was alone.

I still see Mom dressed up in a Pucci-print dress Gramma made her, stepping onto the patio with a tray of something delicious she'd concocted, while Dad, behind the bar, shakes martinis and pours Moscow mules. Do I recall a Twister game at one of their parties? I do remember a bunch of adults in our living room sitting cross-legged at low tables for a luau, my mother wearing a lei of fresh flowers. For one summer bash, Mom and one of her best friends appear in bold-print paper dresses—the latest fad. Bored by the off-color jokes inspired by the disposable dresses, my mother retreats and comes back downstairs in a demure cocktail dress. I'm at her sling-back heels, begging, "Can I wear the paper dress now?" "No!" she snaps. Still, I am impressed by how "with it" she is.

Later, when Mom presents her dessert—Baked Alaska or chocolate fondue?—I peek and watch the guests' faces light up. *Oh, Catherine!* At times like this, my mother seems to me infinitely capable. Though prim and slightly European with her hair in a French twist, she is jaunty with her curlicue bangs and dangling red big-ball earrings—a potent young woman in her prime.

By the time I was in high school, my mother, in my eyes, had failed me. "You want *me* to tell your father to let you go?" Mom said the first time I was asked out on a date. "And if something happens, he'll blame me. Uhn-uh, you fight your own battles with your father. I've got enough problems."

I was on my own. "Dad, *everybody*—"

"When you're 25," he insisted, "when you have a doctor's degree in some field, then it will be time to date. I'll tell you when."

"We're not in Italy," I mouthed off. "It's not 1944." We were in the suburbs of Pittsburgh, and it was the early seventies, and to me, his vigilance felt like callous patriarchal possessiveness, and it was demeaning.

"Why don't you just lie to him?" my friends suggested.

I never did. In part because I wasn't a kid who sneaked. But also, as much as I wanted to go out with that incredibly bad-boy-cute guy from Central Catholic, I was bull-headed in my determination to win my father over to my way of thinking.

As for my mother, I needed to *demonstrate* for her how a female could stand up for herself.

"Look, Dad, what reasons have I given you not to trust me?"

"None," he had to admit. "None, so far." To have a grown man's attention and be able to see on his face that I was making my point—this was heady business, almost better than being allowed to go on the actual date.

My questioning continued. "And why would I want to lose your trust? How would that possibly benefit me?"

In calmer moments, my father advised me, "You should become a lawyer."

The summer after my high school graduation, my mother and I had our most difficult time. Mom, Paul, and I were visiting our family in Calabria, and Mom and I battled daily. (In August, Dad would join us, and then we'd all argue.) It was an existential tug-of-war over my freedom, played out in debates about whether I could go out at night with my cousin, a year older than me, and his friends—particularly the one guy I was falling for. A few of the aunts were confused by the fact that my American parents were more restrictive than the Italians were with their kids. One night, they assured my mother, "It's nearby, dancing, nothing serious!" Before Mom could stop me, the aunts warned my cousin that I was his responsibility—*"Capisci?"*—and whispered to me, *"Vai, vai!"* I slipped into the friend's crowded Fiat 500, and we drove hairpin turns to a dance club carved into the mountains, with terraces looking out over the sea, moonlight glinting on the water, the dance floor lit from below and pulsing under my platform shoes—and my mother had wanted me to *miss this*?

Most of the bickering between Mom and me was public—there were fifteen of us at the beach living in two apartments—but one afternoon we crossed paths in the stairwell and she grabbed my arm. "Listen," Mom said in an urgent whisper, "I came here at 18, just like you, and I thought it was all fun and games, and what happened to me happened, but I'll be hanged if I let that happen to you."

"But that was you, not me," I hissed. "Why'd you marry him if you didn't want to?" She regretted the decision she'd made years earlier, so now she wanted *my* life as compensation? "I'm not you," I said, rushing down the stairs to get away from her. "Leave me alone!"

In September, back from Italy, my family drove me to the only school my father and I could agree on: Saint Mary's College, an all-women's college across the road from Notre Dame University. Within a few days, I had a serious boyfriend, which never would have happened if I were living at home.

Tim was the first guy to tell me *I love you*, and I said it back. Freshman year, I couldn't imagine waiting four years to get married; and yet, as we walked the long, tree-lined road from one campus to the other—in every season that walk was a romantic idyll—I already felt nostalgic for those moments we were living. *This is all too lovely to be real.*

Men weren't allowed in the dorms at Saint Mary's, so Tim and I made out enthusiastically in his room at N.D. Frequently we were interrupted by guys from his floor tossing popcorn or socks through the transom, sometimes they planted tape recorders under the bed. Fun times, but the *Animal House* ambience was not a place where a girl felt comfortable letting loose.

This isn't real life.

My father assumed I'd return to Pittsburgh after college, get a writing job, and eventually marry Tim, whom he liked a lot. Having resigned himself to the American practice of dating, Dad was willing to let a year or two pass as lead-in to a wedding.

Instead, the summer after graduation, I attended a publishing course in Boston and then—breaking my parents' hearts—I moved to Manhattan to interview for jobs.

It was September 1977 and I was 21 years old. The flight from Pittsburgh was just an hour, but my arrival in New York felt as lucky and as monumental to me as it must have for anyone who ever sailed into Ellis Island. In leaving my family's home, I was an anarchist. For Gramma Stella and Nonna Anna, for my mom and my aunts, a life between the home of the father and the home of the husband had never existed.

But now it did exist.

I gazed through the double-paned window of the USAir jet down onto the apartment complexes, the willowy grasses along the shores that hug the runways at LaGuardia, and, enchanted by that harsh beauty, I was thinking, *Please, God, let there be a place for me down there.*

And there was.

The city was completely new to me, yet it felt completely known. I can put it no other way but to say I was happy in my skin.

My parents had reluctantly paid my airfare, assuming I'd return home after a few interviews. When, instead, I stayed, they were sure a great misfortune was falling on our family. Mornings, as I dressed up for job interviews, they'd call my friend's apartment where I was staying, Mom crying and Dad lamenting, "I never thought a daughter of mine would be living *like that*." By the time we hung up and I rushed out, in my navy-blue interview suit, I was in tears. That anyone hired me was a miracle.

Meanwhile, Tim was in the Midwest, in a corporate training program. In time, we'd become lifelong friends, but that autumn there was no way around the fact that we were moving in different directions.

Within a month, I was a PR assistant at Farrar, Straus and Giroux—the prestigious publishing house in scruffy Union Square. I was living in a three-bedroom, three-bathroom apartment with three other recent college grads—all female—in a pre-war doorman building on West 72nd Street, kitty-corner from the Dakota. John Lennon, Yoko Ono, and other luminaries were my neighbors just across the street. I'd arrived when New York City was in a severe downturn, just a few months after the capture of serial killer Son of Sam and not long after the looting and fires following the July blackout. I was naive and didn't realize how crippled the city was. All I knew was that rentals were waiting to be filled, even in prime locations. I was just blocks from Lincoln Center and my father's beloved Metropolitan Opera, but that was no comfort to him. "When are you coming back home?" he demanded.

Caller ID and answering machines didn't exist, so sometimes I simply let the phone ring. I hated hurting them—their daughter alone in New York City really did mark the end of what was acceptable—but I was greedy for my own life. The previous summer, on the beach in Calabria, a family friend had said to me, "*Tu vuoi mangiare tutto il mondo!*" I'd been describing the amorphous career in the arts I hoped to establish—"Writing or editing, maybe in Rome or New York or Chicago; yeah, definitely Rome would be cool"—and that's when he told me, *You want to eat up the whole world!*

He was only an acquaintance, but I felt he'd seen directly into my soul. I knew that, as a modus operandi, my long-range plan was flimsy, but just as the man had said, I was hungry and wanted the world.

Sometimes as I was walking down a random block, I'd stop and think, *Right now, in this moment, on this one street, pretty much any activity a human is capable of—best and worst—might be going on without anyone else knowing*. I was, of course, tantalizing myself with the vast possibilities available to *me* since I had Houdini-ed myself out of suburbia. *I can go anywhere, do anything.* I savored the anonymity of the streets, stared shamelessly when a face in the crowd snagged my attention. Against the backdrop of the city, every stranger's life was potentially an epic. I didn't think of myself as a writer yet, but I was chasing narratives, sometimes following people, eavesdropping on foreign languages, trying to puzzle out someone's story by interpreting the emotional resonance of their speech. One morning, as I walked to the subway, a gun fell out of a guy's jacket pocket and onto the pavement, right at my feet. Quickly he gathered up his gun, tucked it away, blended into the crowd. How many others carried guns on the way to work? Why?

During my first winter, there were two blizzards, and in the dazzling, ice-flecked days after one of those storms, I started dating a filmmaker who would, in time, set the template for the kind of rarefied relationship—romance as artistic collaboration—that I'd seek out and suffer from for years. Our first dates were slow dinners at a tiny Italian restaurant. Talk-talk-talk about books and films. He was a good listener, more serious about making art than making money—a noble person, I thought, and he could be very funny.

Long walks in my neighborhood. The elevator up to my apartment. Brief chitchat with my roommates on the way to my room, where we closed the door. On my turntable, Grover Washington, Jr. played "Jamming." My mattress was on box springs on the hardwood floor; embedded into the decorative baseboards, the fifty-year-old dust of many lives. The filmmaker and I lay below the vaulted ceiling. All night, shouts and sirens filtered in through the leaded windows, and I wondered if any female from my family's Vazzano had ever traveled this far away.

In New York when I was 21, I felt sure I could not die. I'd been cautious in college, kept myself safe, not wanting to squander my luck there. But now it was spring and I was crossing Central Park at midnight, on a work night, in a cab speeding me to the iffy neighborhood where my filmmaker lived. Stuffed into my canvas bag, along with my work clothes for the next day, I had some manuscript or other to show him.

Him! A few years older than me and an experienced writer. By now, he was my first reader and career adviser. He shared his scripts with me, too, so we were collaborators, not just lovers. I had a sense of mission. Destiny had meant for me to live these days, these nights.

As I stepped out of the cab, crunching broken-bottle shards under the soles of my boots, I ran to the vestibule of the filmmaker's building, my heart galloping. Ringing the buzzer for his apartment once, then again, caught in the tight space between the outer door that opened freely to the dark street and the locked inner door that led up to the dubious safety of this man's home, I felt the solitariness you feel in the confessional. When you're alone like that, it's just you there, with your limited strength, with all your sins (like abandonment of loved ones, or greedy grabbing for too much in life), sins that will someday demand a price.

But not yet. There's the click, the door unlocked, then that rush of relief, almost as good as salvation. Spasm of adrenaline, just what's needed to run up the five flights.

And I did run, fast enough to ignore the choking knowledge that I was in so deep, this man could badly break my heart.

But not yet. Tonight he's coming down the steps to meet me, all sweet words and smiling. Tonight we are happy. New York is still doling out only generous, good love. Hadn't the bountiful heavens given me everything I had just to risk it for this?

Risk. How we love our brave selves.

One night, surprisingly early in our relationship, the filmmaker said, "I'm thinking about something with you I never thought about with anyone before." We were lying across his bed this time, in the tiny room with the bars on the windows.

"What?" I asked.

"Marriage," he whispered, and just as I was thinking, *Ah, so this is how it happens*, he quickly added, "but I could never have Catholic children."

We're going to have children together!

But wait: *He doesn't like my family's religion—and possibly, by extension, he doesn't think he'll like my family.*

The filmmaker went on to explain that there'd already been a serious rift in his family when his older brother—an Ivy Leaguer like him, I believe—had married an Italian American woman.

I continued seeing the filmmaker for more than a year, confounded that a certain level of trust eluded us. *What's wrong with me?*

By April 1980, the weeks of a big subway strike, the filmmaker and I had broken up and he was seeing a former friend of mine. I was working at *McCall's*, and each morning, walking the long walk to the Helmsley Building, I indulged in long, noisy fantasies about becoming a rock star—I'd call myself Infanta (Madonna was a rising star) and sing scathing hard-rock versions of Motown hits, like "You Keep Me Hangin' On."

In time, the filmmaker and my former friend married. Many years would pass before I realized how deeply that man had disappointed me. I had accused myself: *I ruined everything. We were going to make movies together, change the world, create!* I convinced myself that *I* was the one who fell short, *I* was the one with the narrow vision.

In time, a smart therapist would tell me, "The way you talk to yourself—you have a Mafia inside of you, terrorizing you. Where do you think that voice came from?"

Chapter 7

Prophetess

> *A second chance, that's the delusion. There never was but one.*
> —"The Middle Years," Henry James

Labor Day weekend, 1980. I was about to begin grad school and had recently moved into a West End Avenue apartment I was sharing with a med student. My bedroom window faced south, and if I leaned out a bit and looked right, I saw a strip of the Hudson River. Slowly, the city, once again, was feeling wide.

During my three years working various nine-to-five publishing jobs, I'd grabbed time during lunch breaks and weekends to work on stories. Craving more time to write, I'd applied to Columbia's MFA creative-writing program. To my shock, I got in. That Labor Day weekend, I felt flush in all the new freedom I'd created for myself.

That same weekend, in Pittsburgh, in my grandparents' new house—they'd finally left Braddock and bought a house about a mile from my parents—Gramma Stella heard a noise in the basement. She found Grampa Joe collapsed at the bottom of the stairs. He'd had a stroke severe enough that he was paralyzed on his left side and mumbling when he tried to speak. He was almost 80.

After his hospital stay, he went to a rehab center. I didn't see him until I went to Pittsburgh for Thanksgiving. By then, he was back home, still had some paralysis, was speaking a bit more clearly, but he was so angry that Gramma confessed she was sometimes afraid of him. "He's still strong in that right arm," she said more than once.

"Afraid of what, Gram?" Even in this extreme situation the husband had the say-so? The most pressing problem, it seemed to me, was that Grampa needed a huge amount of care. "Please," I begged her, "don't try to nurse him by yourself. It's too much. We'll find a good place for him."

"No, no, no, no," she insisted. "He'll think I put him away. What will people say, that without even trying, I sent him to a place?" No matter how robust and supportive a clan of *paesani* is—and ours was and still is very supportive—it's not possible to be part of such a group without internalizing the perceived judgments of the collective. "I couldn't live with myself," she said. "No."

Grampa's hospital bed was set up in their living room, and at night Gramma rolled out the sofa bed so she was nearby when he called for help. She never slept through the night. Now, as she and I talked upstairs in the guest room, Grampa yelled, "Stella! My pills! I'm having pain."

"Okay, Joe!" she yelled back. To me, she said, "It's the sickness talking." Earlier, though, she'd said she felt afraid. I could understand *furious* or *exhausted*, but why *afraid*?

We were lying across the bed. I had on a peach-colored slip and Gramma had straight pins pinned to her collar because she'd just measured the hem of a new dress she was making for me. I can still see her hand flat on the bedspread between us, her fingers tapping at the petals of a chenille daisy. She leaned on her elbow, resting her head in her other hand, while her gaze shifted from me to the ceiling as she called on the saints. "*Sa'brancisco*, please, if only you'd let him walk."

The new dress was for Christmas in Italy. My parents and I were going to visit my brother, who was studying architecture in Rome, and then we'd travel to Calabria together for the holiday with our relatives, a long-held family dream. I'm shocked now that we didn't cancel that trip, and more shocked that I didn't take that dress from my grandmother and say, "Don't worry about this now. Rest."

What I did say: "Gramma, would Grampa do this for you?" All the freedom in my New York life—I wanted it for Gramma, too. "You've got to think about yourself," I insisted, as if feminist rhetoric could dampen age-old mandates.

Gramma had a cynical way of pursing her lips—easier to accept misery than to believe there was a choice.

I grabbed her hand. "Promise me that if having Grampa home doesn't get easier soon, you'll try something else."

She smirked. "I promise you nothing." She sat up. "We'll see." She rubbed the chalk marks off the hem of my dress.

"Oh, *Stel*-la!"

"I'm coming, Joe!" she yelled. To me, she said, "How soon do you need this dress?"

Four months later, in March, Grampa was moved into "a place" because Gramma was in intensive care with congestive heart failure. When my parents called me to come home, my mother warned, "Listen, Gramma said to tell you not to come here saying, 'I told you so.' She said not to give her a hard time, you hear me?"

Of course, Grampa's nursing home was a sad place, but nothing was as heartbreaking as seeing Gramma Stella propped up in the ICU holding an oxygen mask over her mouth, struggling to breathe. For five months, she'd been Grampa's full-time caregiver. She had known she had a slight heart ailment, but it was mild compared with my mother's lifelong illness, which had always been front and center for Gramma. She was mother, counselor, and best friend for Catherine, and always available for all of us. When I saw Gramma in the hospital, she had lost so much weight, she was half her normal size. And in my eyes, our family had also become a puny thing. When we got home from visiting hours each night, my parents and I had conversations about where Gramma should go when she was discharged.

"She should come to our house and stay as long as she needs to," I insisted.

"And who's going to take care of her? Your mother isn't able to." That was my father, hiding behind my mother's illness.

"Your father doesn't want her here, do you understand that?" That was my mother, speaking the truth, but only after my father had left the kitchen. It's not that my father didn't care about Gramma Stella; actually, she and Dad enjoyed each other a lot. But if Gramma lived at our house, Grampa Joe would end up there, too. Though civil to each other, my father and grandfather were not comfortable in each other's company. Long ago, they'd had some peasant-type misunderstanding that none of them would ever discuss. But weren't we far beyond that Old World business? Family is family.

I did consider moving home to help, taking a leave from my grad program, but my parents said, "No! School is where you belong."

I have to be honest. I did not want to return to Pittsburgh. If I did, I'd likely be swallowed up by my family for the rest of my life. I had grabbed a lot of liberty when I left home and moved to New York, and I didn't want to give any of it back.

Coward. I was a coward.

Gramma was released from the hospital on her 66th birthday, April 2, and that weekend I flew home. My mother set the table with the good china, as she did for celebratory occasions, and there was cake. Gramma reminded us that she had been born on Good Friday. Laughing, she said, "Maybe that brought me my bad luck."

"You're not unlucky, Gram. Don't say that."

"You know," she said, looking at me significantly, "I *was* born with a veil over my face."

"What does that mean?" I thought the image of a newborn's veiled face was poetic, suggesting she'd entered the world as pure as a young bride, bringing an untainted life force with her, but I was wrong.

"Prophetess," Gramma told me, with her eyes wide. "That's what it means."

My father explained, "What they called 'the veil' was the afterbirth. Sometimes if it covered the face of the baby, the midwives said it was an omen, that the child would be a person who could tell the future. Superstitions," he scoffed.

I ignored my father and asked my grandmother, "You think it's true you could see the future?"

She raised her eyebrows. She wasn't going to contradict my father, but she wasn't conceding either. "Who knows? Funny things have happened to me."

*

Over the next months, we all were mystified as her face transformed, her translucent skin accordioned into infinitesimal wrinkles. Her strong shoulders collapsed. When we fussed over her, she smiled at us because she knew what we wanted, but her smiles hung briefly on her cheeks, passed quickly through her eyes, left them empty of joy, haunted with questions, almost a reproach, a look so unnerving my mother said, half-joking, half-not, "Don't look at me like that! I don't know what to do for you." None of us could take away the hurt from Gramma's eyes as she slowly realized that somehow she'd been duped.

In New York, I lived within a few blocks of my closest friends. When any of us was brought low by lovers or bosses, we'd gather, offer distraction. We shared the credo that as long as your friends can help you, you don't need therapy. In those days, I thought therapy was nothing but the punch line of a *New Yorker* cartoon. But back at school, as my family's crisis continued, I wasn't doing well. One sweaty spring Sunday, the temperature over eighty, I took a drastic risk during my weekly phone call with my parents. On my bedroom floor, I was stretched out, a five-point star in surrender. From below my window, the neighborhood ice-cream truck was imposing its cloying singsong. And then I just came out with it, sure that, once again, I was taking our family in a shocking new direction. "I think I'm depressed," I told them. "I may need to talk to a therapist." I expected the Earth to change the course of its rotation.

But I'd overestimated my role as maverick. I was shocked to hear my father say, "Yes, well, we were going to tell you, your mother has begun to see a psychiatrist. Her doctor recommended it for her upset over your grandmother's illness." Dad's voice combined his professional gravitas with the halting reserve of a shameful admission.

For both my mother's sake and my own, I knew what I had to say next. "Mom, this is good. It's brave." I had no idea yet how therapy worked. "Is it scary?"

She laughed, sort of. "No. It's good to talk, it helps." Now and then, my mother and I had moments when we were in sync. For example, here we were, both falling apart.

In late summer, my brother and I were in Pittsburgh. In between hospital stays—there were several—Gramma was living at our house, all of us in an air-conditioned holding pattern, still committed to the hope she'd somehow recover. Before Paul and I took off again, my mother wanted to take a family photo.

It was evening, just after sunset. The humidity had lifted and the light was sharp. My mother and I quickly changed into dresses, and we all gathered in the backyard. The grass was deep green and plush. Long columns of light fell through tall evergreens. My father, an enthusiastic amateur photographer, was focusing the lens of his camera, which was perched on a tripod. "This time of day," he said, "the light is a little tricky."

It's magic hour, I thought. That patch of time between dusk and nightfall that filmmakers love. I'd learned the phrase from my filmmaker. I'd never told anyone, not even Gramma, what he'd said about having Catholic children. He did join me once for a visit to Pittsburgh. When I asked Gramma what she thought of him, she paused. "I'm sorry, dear, but I have to say I think no. He's not good for you." She saw right through that relationship's magic hour.

Now, as Dad was setting up the self-timer, Gramma stood up from the patio glider and walked out onto the grass. She wasn't in much pain that day, and she told him, "I'll take the picture." Dad joined us, and as we posed, Gram stood looking into the viewfinder for a long time. Maybe she was trying to center us perfectly? Or she wanted to hold us there all together?

"Ma," my mother said, "tell us if it's too much standing, you hear?"

"Pronti?" Gramma said in her sharpest Italian, and finally she clicked the camera. Later, in the prints, we'd see that none of us was smiling.

"Stand in a different place," Gramma said. "I'll take more."

We posed next to my father's rosebushes, and in front of the tallest evergreen, and then Paul said, "Let's take one with you, Gramma."

"For the love of God, no, no." She left the lawn, stood at the sliding glass door.

"Sure, Gramma, come on," I said. She used to love getting everyone into family pictures.

Without a word, she slipped inside.

From our family photo session in the backyard during Gramma's last summer, not one shot was enlarged and framed. In each photo, either my brother or I looked grim, our mother looked worried, or we all looked as if we were watching something disturbing. And we were. Nothing so clearly records the horror we felt about Gramma's deteriorating health as those photos of us watching her as she photographed us.

Gramma got a lot of phone calls, often from her former work friends. She'd been almost 50 when she began working at Saks Fifth Avenue doing alterations, mostly on silks. Grampa had been sick with cancer and couldn't work in the bar, and so Gramma had no choice. He hated the idea of her working outside the house. "I didn't send you," he screamed. "You don't need to go to a job!"

But she did have to go. They needed the income. She got her first ID card and a monthly bus pass. She had her paycheck—sort of.

"I never got to keep one paycheck," she told Paul and me as we sat out on the glider with her. That summer, with Grampa in the nursing home, Gramma talked more freely than she had before. "Your grandfather yelled, 'Give me the check! It goes in the bank!' What good does that do me now that I'm sick?"

During her fifteen years at Saks, she was finally out in the world daily, in the heart of downtown Pittsburgh, walking the city blocks of chunky old buildings. Horne's, Gimbels, and Kaufmann's department stores. Jenkins Arcade, with its fancy shops for luggage, furs, and china, and that little place that sold nothing but buttons. Bank buildings, movie theaters, lunch counters. She loved the flower vendors on the street, and for my 14th birthday, she brought me my first bouquet of roses. But she also became familiar with traffic jams, slush in the crosswalks in winter, manhole covers steaming in summer. City life.

When she started the job, Gramma had to buy herself a cheap wedding ring because her original band no longer fit and, working downtown, she had to reassure Grampa she wasn't "giving anybody any ideas." She wasn't bragging; the ring was one more effort to calm down her husband. All the years she worked, she could never let Grampa think she enjoyed it.

I think she did enjoy it. I visited her at work, met her friends, most of them immigrants from Italy, Russia, Poland. One woman in the sewing room had a concentration-camp number tattooed on her forearm. A few times I caught the bus home with Gramma. We stood in the crowded aisle, walked that last stretch of road, and I saw what goes into a full workday. Years later, when students asked me how to complete a novel, I told them, "Punch in every morning, punch out at the end of the day. Put in the hours. If you can have some laughs in the workroom, that's a bonus."

Late summer, I had to leave Pittsburgh to begin the fall semester, and Mom's psychiatrist gave me the number for a New York psychiatrist. I moved the scrap of paper with his phone number from one pile to another but didn't call, even though, as I walked down Broadway after classes, I was often crying behind my sunglasses. *Gramma is dying because of Grampa's stroke.* It was unspeakably unfair.

The psychiatrist's name was Dr. T and his office was on 86th Street near Fifth, but from the start I called him Howard, to drain a little authority from him. He was extremely tall—taller than necessary, it seemed to me.

"Can you put words to your anger?" he asked when I began seeing him.

You idiot! "Listen," I'd tell him at the start of the session, "I think this isn't helping me." When my time was up, though, I'd panic. "The hour's over, and we didn't get anything done! Nothing's changed, nothing's better!"

Gently, he asked, "Is this how it feels when it's time to leave your family at the end of a visit?"

"How should I know?" Then, quiet admission: "Yeah, I guess it is."

"I thought so," he said.

"Meaning?"

"That it's easier to leave angry." This was the first useful thing I heard Howard say.

One night, late, my parents called. "It's your decision," Mom said, "but Gramma's in the hospital, and it doesn't look good."

The next day, I flew to Pittsburgh. As I sat on Gramma's hospital bed, she was smiling. During the night, she'd suffered one of her worst bouts of pain, but with the morning she was on the other side of it.

"You had us so scared." Mom and her cousins laughed the grateful laugh of relief.

"Maybe I just needed to see my grandchild." Gramma smiled at me. I'm sure I was holding her hand.

Later, when it was just the two of us, Gramma said to me slowly, out of nowhere, "You know what I want?"

"What, Gramma?"

"I want to write the story of my life."

A moment of silence passed between us. To this day, I believe I understood her correctly.

"All the things that happened to me," she said, "that story."

"I can help you with that," I told her.

"Yeah," she said. "You do it."

The following afternoon, on the way to the airport, I stopped at the hospital again. Gramma was sitting up in her bed, her hair smoothly combed and braided. She'd just eaten lunch; she'd had some appetite. I kissed her. We hugged.

But when I got to the door, I turned and looked at her. Something made me go back to hug her a second time. And then I broke every rule I'd made for myself—*do not cry, do not let her think you don't believe she'll recover*—and I began weeping as hard as I ever have in my life. I knew I'd never see my grandmother alive again.

"Everything will be okay, dear," she said as she held me. "It's in God's hands."

Three weeks later, the night my parents called to tell me Gramma had died, after I finally fell asleep, I dreamed of her. In my dream, Gramma was young, healthy, beautiful, dressed in a bright-blue sleeveless dress, showing her strong arms, smiling. When I mentioned the dream to my cousins at the funeral home, they told me, "That was your gramma letting you know she's free now and feels good." A lovely interpretation, but I knew that Gramma had died before she'd had a chance to set things right.

I knew this because there was another dream, a recurring one I'd had on those summer nights when she was at our house. In that dream, it was night, and my family and I were gathered with a large crowd on a city street, looking up at a high-rise window. As everyone watched, a woman jumped from the window, falling slowly, but at the end, landing heavily. The crowd couldn't save her; we had simply watched.

"Now, why did she do that?" Grampa, indignant, asked in the dream, at which point Gramma silently walked away, and Grampa asked, "Now, where is *she* going?"

Over her cotton housedress, Gramma was wearing a trench coat, and she walked fast. I followed. "Gramma, Gramma!" The most startling aspect of the dream was that she wasn't making it easy for me to catch up with her. This was contrary to how I'd ever known her. I chased her. She was rushing down the subway steps at Broadway and 96th Street, the station closest to my apartment. Pushing through turnstiles, I called, "Gramma!" She wasn't running, just walking fast, fed up with all of us.

Every time I had this dream, I woke up panicked. The woman had jumped from the window. We had watched a suicide. And, in fact, calmly, for years, we had watched Gramma absorb all kinds of pain; and now, innocently, we asked, "Hey, how come?"

But Gramma, in the dream, had not died; she walked away with an emphatic sense of purpose. Independent and self-protective; hence, the trench coat.

All day after that recurring dream, I'd hurt. Gramma's attitude suggested there was nothing I could do to help her, and nothing she'd be able to do for me. *Each of us is on her own.*

"Your grandmother," Howard said when I told him that dream, "is one of your spiritual advisers."

I hadn't begun to trust him yet, but I thought it was smart of him to invite my grandmother into the room.

Chapter 8

The Courtyard

> *Our very life depends on everything's*
> *Recurring till we answer from within.*
> *The thousandth time may prove the charm.—That leaf!*
>   —"Snow," Robert Frost

Before she died, Gramma had told me, "I want to write the story of my life," and I felt an urgent obligation to chronicle, in fiction, what had happened to her—to our whole family—in Italy and America. In draft after draft, I entered our story from different angles, but something eluded me, even after I spent three months doing research in Italy.

In Rome, I had rented a tiny rooftop apartment above Largo Arenula, in the heart of the old city. My uncle loaned me his Olivetti manual typewriter, but Rome is a city for walking, so I spent a good part of each day outside, taking notes. One hot autumn afternoon, I stepped off a busy street, into the shaded entry of a monastery that led into an ancient courtyard. Quiet. Water dripped in a stone fountain, and the thought came to me this way: To be a woman in an Italian family, *my* family, is to live in a courtyard, an enclosed world—it is safety, confinement, beauty, deprivation, fulfillment, wretched, wonderful, inescapable. After that day, I couldn't stop writing about courtyards. By the time I left Rome, I had an organizing metaphor for my story.

But back in New York, a year later, I was still unable to carve a narrative arc from my avalanche of notes. I was stuck.

In every area of life, stuck. Writing, romance, my weekly (at times, twice a week) sessions with Howard. I'd begun therapy when Gramma's illness cracked our family open, anticipating that after a month or two of unburdening myself I'd arrive at a resolution. But as I worked with Howard (and it *was* work), my anger widened and my sadness deepened. Reflecting on my grandmother's life, I became increasingly aware of every patriarchal injustice ever committed against woman or man. Powered by new insight, pulsing, I'd rush home to my manuscript, but the chapters and scenes, and even the sentences, pushed back at me. *Stuck, so stuck!* My biggest disadvantage was that I hadn't learned my family's full story yet, but I didn't know that. At one point, I put the manuscript in a drawer and spent the summer reading *War and Peace*. Maybe I'd learn something by osmosis.

My ongoing sorrow made no sense. I was doing the work I wanted to do, living in the city I'd fought to bring myself to, but there was no peace in it, no satisfaction.

My father tried to be helpful: "Perhaps you can choose a career different than writing?"

"Dad, don't!"

My relations with my parents were still fraught. We'd never found peace around the shock of Gramma's illness and death. Then, four years later, we lost Grampa. Without the filter of my grandparents' presence, my parents and I were forced into tighter emotional proximity. My brother and I were close, but, like a lot of siblings, we'd had very different childhood experiences. We had the same parents, but marriage didn't frighten Paul. In fact, he'd married young, and he and his wife had moved to Chicago.

Meanwhile, I lived in New York and my parents were in Pittsburgh, but there was little air between us.

"And still you see that psychiatrist?"

"I've got to go now, Dad. I'll talk to you later."

As my therapy intensified, my serial romances were dramatic and followed a pattern: attraction to connection, connection to ruptured trust, ruptured trust to heartbreak and to an extra session with Howard. Somehow I had come to the warped conclusion that romance was not an end in itself but rather a sort of internship in service to therapy.

One boyfriend accused me: "Therapy is like a secular religion for you."

"That's not true at all," I told him. "Not at all," I repeated, because he was correct.

Walking to my session, depending on where I was coming from,

I'd sometimes pass a modern high-rise at Park Avenue and 79th Street. This apartment building was so upscale, notable sculptures were installed outside its front door. For a while, Henry Moore's "Interconnecting Figures" was featured. It was replaced by Francisco Zuniga's stunning "Four Generations," a sculpture of four peasant women standing with their undisciplined bellies protruding, their heads capped in veils. Each woman faced a different direction. Together, they covered the compass's full range, and I let myself think that, like the *comare* of Vazzano, Zuniga's women had my back. I felt affection for them as they stood, bold and unapologetic, at that elite intersection. I imagined them telling me, *They planted us here among these rich people, so clearly, we belong, and you do, too.* But I could also hear them admonish me: *Okay, we're doing our part, now you—you're the one with the words. Go to Howard's office, get to work!*

"You need to separate from your family." Every time Howard said that, I felt he was pushing me toward some psychological imperative I wasn't sure I wanted to achieve. I'd broken my parents' hearts when I moved to New York. How ruthless did I have to be before I became my fully realized self? As earnestly as I worked with Howard, every time he suggested that my parents and I weren't adequately "separated," I'd look at him, gentle giant of a therapist, and think, *You over-tall Northerner.*

"We're Italian," I told him more than once, "we don't do separation."

Often I felt that Howard and I, for all our good intentions, were caught in a cultural impasse we couldn't translate our way out of. Because I could not visualize—let alone realize—the vaulted state of "separation from family," I began to feel again that old shame. In junior high, my Italian hair wasn't straight enough; in high school, I wasn't tall enough. Now, I wasn't psychologically evolved enough.

As I sat or lay on Howard's brown leather couch, I'd stare up at his map of Paris hanging on the wall above me and study the portioned-out arrondissements. Which portions of *me* were, like the neighborhoods of Paris, more desirable than others and which were lesser? Which parts needed to be improved or thoroughly annexed, razed, abandoned?

The peasant parts, perhaps? Or the doctor's indulged daughter? The cliché single woman who, according to a much-publicized study of the time, had a better chance of being killed by a terrorist bomb than of getting married? Perhaps it was time to trounce the writer who, after years of research and revision, couldn't finish her novel. Five years had passed since I'd first come to this map, this couch, this therapist, who sat regally in his high-back leather chair, but still I couldn't figure out where I'd gone wrong. I wasn't fixed yet.

One thing I did have going for me was a terrific part-time job working twelve-hour overnight shifts on Fridays and Saturdays in the Copy Room of *Time* magazine. The job included health insurance that covered a lot of my therapy expenses, and I had time during the week to write. Still, I needed to supplement my income, so I began teaching English as a Second Language at the New York Association for New Americans (NYANA), a resettlement agency for Jewish refugees from the Soviet Union.

My students were engineers, doctors, and professors now training to be manicurists and limo drivers. They were parents and grandparents. Squeezed into tight school desks, they were worn out from months-long travel across the globe and sleepy after their subway treks from Brooklyn. Most were hopeful, though the women, in general, were more positive than the men, who seemed to be struggling against an air of defeat. Anti-Semitism had made it impossible for my students to live and work in their native country, and now they were reliant on social services to help them build a new life. NYANA guided them toward housing, employment, and medical care, and offered intensive daily English-language classes. My job was to introduce the students to the verbs *to be* and *to have*.

"Do you have a VCR?" I'd prompt, following the school's pedagogical method.

"*Yyesss,*" they'd recite as their part in the drill, "I have a VCR."

"Does your neighbor have a VCR?"

"*Yyesss,* my neighbor is a VCR."

We laughed a lot. On their journey to New York, most had resided a few months in Ladispoli, a beach town outside of Rome. When English failed us, we spoke Italian.

My class roster included husbands and wives, in-laws, and adult children and their parents. Meeting them in family clusters, I imagined my students were living some version of the life I would have lived if I hadn't bolted from home at seventeen. I studied them, wondering what they knew about the give-and-take of domestic life that I hadn't figured out yet. I remember a young woman I'll call Tanya. She sat in the far left row, and her husband sat at the desk in front of her; they wore their wedding bands as naturally as tattoos. Though they'd sit through class without acknowledging each other, theirs seemed an easy silence, with no pique in it. At break time, the couple walked wordlessly out of the room together with a pack of cigarettes. Both were around my age; married seven years, they had two sons. How, exactly, had they achieved the level of trust needed to accomplish that? When he went silent on her, did she worry that in America he'd met someone new? When she was aloof, did he wonder if she was writing letters to some guy back in Tbilisi? I couldn't envision marriage without sketching in danger, betrayal, fear. What would have made it possible for Gramma to resist Grampa's prohibition and come to a class like this one to learn English?

During the year I taught at NYANA, I got a glimpse of the damage suffered when a whole population is robbed of power, stripped. And I also saw up close how, if an individual wants to take power back, they need to dip into a reserve of extraordinary strength, an inner force that must be mammoth and unrelenting, something like a blast furnace or an oncoming subway train.

"Do you have a kitchen in your apartment?"

"*Yyesss*, I have big chicken in my apartment."

One day I had to leave early for a dental appointment. The next day when I returned, the class was unusually quiet, almost somber. "What's up?" I asked.

One man gravely volunteered: "You go to dentist, and we are betrayed."

When I told Howard that story, he smiled at me for a long time. He shook his head and said, "And you tell me there's no love in your life." He was right. There was much good, and I was taking it for granted. But soon I'd be turning 30.

And then it was the night of my 30th. A friend threw me a party. Afterward, at home, I lay for hours on my couch—actually, Gramma's dusty couch that I'd dragged to Manhattan from Braddock, along with her Depression-era kitchen set and a cedar chest full of dresses and suits she'd made. Those treasures helped me feel surrounded by family. But tonight, agitated, I stared out the window at the constellation of city lights, thinking, *I've squandered my best chances.*

Close to dawn, in a fit of delayed adolescence and dropping the facade of confident independence I tried to maintain during calls with my parents, I dialed their number, knowing I was waking them, knowing I was making myself ridiculous. "I'm 30," I told them, "and I'm not getting anything right." My phone was tucked into my sweaty neck, my nightgown stale. "Nothing's building. I'm failing at everything."

And my father, God bless him, took the high road. Refraining, uncharacteristically, from lecturing me on the ways I might have done things differently, he told me I was still young and I would be okay. And then, in an act of generosity for which I'll be forever grateful, he told me that when he was 30, he, too, was struggling. This from a man who rarely admitted to weakness, error, or regret. "I was in Yonkers," he said, "I couldn't speak English. I had to start my career again from nothing. In Italy, I was a doctor, and now I was an intern living in student housing." *In a dormitory, at 30?* He went on to say he was "making so little money, your mother and I couldn't even live together. She had to stay in Braddock with her parents."

What caught my attention was "your mother and I couldn't even live together," which stated outright that he had *wanted* to be with her. By then, the deep strain in my parents' marriage was an established fact that puzzled me as much as it hurt me to watch. Two good people capable of great affection and kindness, clearly committed to staying together, yet they were turned away from each other as if some ugly obstacle had been forced between them. It was almost a child's relief I felt when I heard my father's regret: *We couldn't even live together.*

After decades of watching my parents disappoint each other, I still wanted to believe theirs was a love match. I wanted that for them, because otherwise, how would I find it for myself?

Chapter 9

Easter

> *It was a big and solid shadow, and it looked so much like my mother that I became frightened. For I could not be sure whether for the rest of my life I would be able to tell when it was really my mother and when it was really her shadow standing between me and the rest of the world.*
> —"Somewhere, Belgium," Jamaica Kincaid

Your mother and I couldn't even live together. My father's admission meant a lot to me, and I held it close. I didn't bring it up with my mother until a few years later, in spring 1992, while sitting with her on the beach in Florida, where they'd recently retired. She was 61. Dad had just turned 72 and had survived two heart attacks and bypass surgery. How I wished that at this juncture they'd be able to make a new start, change the tenor of their rapport. But as my mother settled into her beach chair and I stretched out on my towel, she began reciting all the ways Dad was driving her crazy, now more than ever. "Everything I do bothers him," she told me. "If I'm on the phone, he's got something to say about it. If I watch my TV shows, he doesn't like it."

"Mom, ignore the small stuff. You're living in this beautiful place. You got through his surgery. You're both here, you're together."

"Together, my foot."

My mother was quiet in her chair next to me, but I could feel her coiled anger. Should she have left my father years ago, when she dragged my brother and me down to our grandparents', or had she been wise to stay married? Two years had passed since Sam and I had ended our engagement. If I'd had more courage, would I still be with

Sam? Or, if we had married, would I have ended up as unhappy as my mother?

"Mom, why didn't you go to Yonkers when Dad left for that job?" I hadn't known I was going to ask that until the words left my mouth. "He said he wanted you with him."

"Oh, give me a break, he *never* said—"

I turned toward her. "He did. He said so. On the phone. It was my birthday, when I turned 30 and I called, he said—"

"Yeah, I know what he says," and then she launched into a version of the Yonkers story that was quite different from anything I'd heard before. In her telling, my father's departure from Braddock a month after their big church wedding had little to do with his urgent need for a job. Their five-year separation was *not* due to her illness and his paltry income. "That's what he wants you to believe."

The truth, she told me, was that a feud had erupted between him and Grampa Joe, and that's why my father had left for Yonkers. "Your father and his family got their noses out of twitch because they said my father was supposed to buy him a car in America. What did he need a car for? He didn't even know how to drive." The heat of my mother's anger could have melted the sand.

"A car?" I asked, rising up on my elbows. "A *car*?"

"They said that Daddy"—how I hated when she called her father *Daddy*, how willingly she embraced that infantilized position—"told them that Alfred would be able to be a doctor in America, no problem. Why would my father tell them that? What did he know about getting a medical license? He owned a beer garden."

My towel was crumpled under me. In the sky now were more clouds than sun, and I dug my hands and feet deep into the sand, trying to find warmth as I pressed her: "What did a car have to do with this?"

My mother was sitting up in her chair. "The streets were lined with gold in Braddock, that's what they thought back in Vazzano. And I'm the dummy who marries him, so he could come to America. Don't get me started."

But she was started.

I listened.

*

The story my mother told me that day about her five-year separation from my father was so shocking, so laced with her hurt and anger, that every Easter since then, and often when I'm sitting on a beach, I remember our conversation. Before I heard her story, I believed our family had been shaped by noble sacrifices made so my father could help his family. Afterward, I understood we were, at base, shaped by something much less grand: a feud that involved cars and money—in essence, a dowry. If *arranged marriage* was distasteful to me, *dowry* made the whole thing vile.

My mother was proposed to because she offered the chance for U.S. citizenship *and a car*? My father argued with my grandfather because he'd married my mother and expected *a car*? I was born of a deal that involved *a car*?

"What was promised in the dowry?" I asked.

"I. Have. No. Idea." Either no one spelled it out for her or they did and she wasn't listening. In which stone-floored room, around whose table with the demitasse cups of espresso were the family members gathered when the deal was spelled out? The bride and groom would not have been present. I can't imagine it was only the parents, because Alfredo's mother, as a female and a widow, would not have negotiated on her own. Mostly I wonder, *Where was Catherine when her marriage was being arranged?*

And later, after her church wedding, why didn't she go with her husband to Yonkers, even if it meant renting a room in someone's attic? The feud was between the men, not between husband and wife.

"I visited him after he left for New York," she told me on the beach. "I brought my suitcases and was ready to move. There I was, and he wouldn't even come see me at that rooming house where I stayed. Every day, I'd wait. I'd go to the soda fountain for a milkshake, and that's what I lived on. Your grandmother was so worried I'd get sick."

"Why didn't you just go to the hospital to see him?"

"Did you *hear* me?" Her voice rose, mixing with the cries of seagulls, forcing me to look at her as she insisted, "He didn't want to see me." She was as furious as if it had happened just that morning.

"I have a diary, and I wrote everything that happened in those five years, and I'm leaving it for *you*." Why did *I* have to be the keeper of her messy emotions? Why not my brother? "Someday you'll read that diary and you'll see who your father is."

She believed she was giving me useful information, perhaps a harsh intervention to help lower my expectations of marriage. Or maybe to help me forget Sam? But she was also getting back at my father. For what?

"You'll read, you'll see what happened!"

How gorgeously her skin tanned and what vibrancy that dark glow gave her. A stranger would never have imagined she was chronically ill. Her profile—the long, fine line of her nose, her high cheekbones—suggested intelligence, authority. It was too much of a stretch to connect this woman who sat next to me with her story of powerlessness. On the outside, Mom was the lovely incarnation of smoothed-out American style. She had a slew of bathing suits, and she looked good in each one. That day she was probably wearing her white lace cover-up and a visor to match her swimsuit. To my eyes, she'd always "looked American." Inside my mother, though, was an Old World syndicate that never stopped charting grudges, testing loyalties. Within her, love moved along paths that were as treacherous as the Calabrian soil where she'd been born. Trust was nearly impossible to come by. If you were foolish enough to trust, you did so at your own peril.

Usually I avoided long talks with my mother, and I could have cut short her disclosures that Sunday, but I sat still, gathering evidence to take to my next therapy session. The panic I'd felt as I turned 30 hadn't abated; rather, sadness was the landscape and weather of my day. Still, I believed I could recover my resilience and was working in therapy more seriously than I had on my English major in college. As much as I wanted to walk away from my mother's story, I stayed put, running sand through my hands, clutching tiny seashells between my toes. "So what happened in Yonkers," I asked as I wrapped my beach towel tighter around me, "after he wouldn't see you?"

"I packed my suitcase and called Uncle Jim to come get me. And that was it."

"For five *years*?"

"I'd write him letters, he never answered."

I had to look away, let this news settle. What was I supposed to do? How to help her? Given the damage, the logical course of action was divorce, but she wasn't saying she wanted that. Within a few hours, we'd sit with my father for our traditional Easter meal. Having told me her tale, she expected me to pretend I'd never heard it. My mother's story trapped me.

But she had more to tell. "Like an idiot, I sent him gifts, and he'd return them."

"He returned your *gifts*?" This was the point in her story when my father turned inexcusably cruel, a man I didn't know at all.

The tide had been rising when we began talking, and we'd had to stand and move to higher ground, closer to the ridge of scruffy dunes. Shark's teeth were abundant on that beach. People made their way across the sand slowly—stopping, bending, collecting. It was a seaside where grandparents hosted and indulged their grandchildren.

Occasionally on this beach, there'd be an outbreak of red tide, a harmful algal bloom. Sea plants produced toxins that sent dying fish up onto the shore, carpeting the sand with decomposing carcasses. The air became so depleted of oxygen, the TV weather reports warned people with asthma and other respiratory illnesses to stay inside. Listening to my mother's story, I strained to breathe, as if a red tide had suddenly infected the air.

Dad had always been my more dependable parent, but today she'd laid it on, dethroned him, scene by scene. "How'd you send him gifts?" I asked. "How'd you know his address if he wasn't in touch with you?" If she was asking me to revise my understanding of the man who was my father, she needed to confirm her details.

"Somehow we always knew. Who can remember, it's been so many years."

So, please, let go of it. Let go.

But how could she? I may have felt trapped by her story, but my mother was bound and imprisoned by it. There wasn't a thing I could say to convince her she was no longer the defenseless 19-year-old cardiac patient not strong enough to wage her own battles. A lovesick bride left to shrivel in those hollow rooms above the bar, while the ambitious, conniving Italian doctor got "just what he wanted!" She was convinced she'd married for love—pure love—while "he knew *exactly* what he was doing!"

We were silent awhile. Quietly, she said, "He was trying to find a way to bring all his family to America." As if this were a bad thing.

"Well, you wanted him to stay in Pittsburgh so you could be near your mother and father. That's what everybody wanted."

"You always see his side, don't you?"

It was true, it was easier to be my father's daughter than it was to be hers. Whenever she insisted on being the victim—*his* victim—I defended him. Was that the imp of the perverse in me? Or was it my need for narrative balance, insisting on two sides for every story? *How could it be bad that he wanted to help his family?*

Watching waves inch up and then away from us, we sat for a long time. Easter was almost over. She'd managed to get me to cry, though I usually didn't give her that satisfaction. Finally I said, "It was lousy what happened between you two, Mom. I'm sorry you had to go through that. But you've had lots of advantages from your marriage, too. And lots of good luck. You have kids, you—"

"Don't you dare think I wasn't happy to have you and your brother. I wanted you and Paul more than anything."

"I know that." Her complaints about her marriage often crescendoed into reassurance that she was grateful to have two children and happy that her children were my brother and me. I always felt sure my mother loved me, even when it seemed we didn't like each other much.

"I went through a lot to have you kids. You *know* that's why I had my operation."

I'd heard many times about her first open-heart surgery, in 1953, which had been so experimental, she was featured in the *Pittsburgh Sun-Telegraph*. She and my father were separated at the time, and she went through the surgery without him, but she was determined to have children, even though doctors warned her that childbirth would be high-risk. When I was in my early 20s, she'd even told me that when she got pregnant with me, doctors had suggested she consider abortion. She'd offered this information to make clear how serious her illness was and to underscore how much she'd wanted children, but the news made me wonder whether it had been her physical or emotional frailty that had prompted her doctors to mention abortion. Could they tell that Catherine's marriage was half-baked? To hear that I'd almost been aborted, that I almost *wasn't*, was not reassuring. My mother's unleashing of confidences, her efforts to create intimacy, often left me feeling squeamish and wanting to run.

But that Easter on the beach she had pinned me down, so I dug in. "If he wasn't in Pittsburgh for your surgery," I asked, "where was he?"

"Who knows? Chicago or Washington. One of those places." My father's far-flung career path was a thread in our family lore, but as my mother unspooled her story, what struck me was how shockingly far apart my parents' lives had been during those five years—separated by hundreds of miles and a canyon of disappointment. What an astonishing distance they'd had to bridge to give birth to two children.

Were there other women when he was out in the world? If I had to guess, I'd say no—we are a family of rule-followers. But probably Catherine's decades-old anger was fueled by even the *possibility* of infidelity. In her view, men were pretty much guilty until they were proved innocent.

"So how'd you get to Joliet?" I knew that Joliet, Illinois, was where she had joined him in the summer of 1955. I was born the following April. Now it hit me that when I was born, my parents weren't just a young couple getting to know each other again, practically strangers— they were bruised strangers. Alfredo had ignored her calls, letters, and gifts, and she was enraged and humiliated, but she still wanted the marriage badly enough to swallow her pride, travel to Joliet, and lock in the deal by getting pregnant.

Pregnancy was the ace up her sleeve. I was born to salvage her marriage—a utilitarian baby who served a purpose, just as her marriage had been arranged to serve a purpose.

Throughout Catherine's early pregnancy in Joliet, there'd been worries about her health. In November, Alfredo, now a U.S. citizen, became a commissioned officer of the U.S. Army Reserve and got orders to report to Army Medical Service School at Fort Sam Houston on January 1. Catherine returned to Braddock to be cared for by her parents.

I was 6 weeks old when my mother and I flew to Fort Benning, and my parents set up housekeeping on the base. "Your father," my mother told me on the beach, "said to go live with him in Fort Benning, but I wasn't allowed"—*not allowed* was embedded in her—"to have any contact with my mother and father. No phone calls. Nothing." Telling this part, she cried. Though she *wasn't allowed* to communicate with her mother, Catherine confided in a neighbor and asked her to call Gramma Stella collect now and then, just so Gramma would know that Catherine and I were okay. Sniffling, full of self-pity, she told me, "That was the only way I could be in touch with my mother."

"Are you nuts?" I sat bolt upright on my beach towel. "Why didn't you just pick up the phone yourself and call Gramma?"

"And let him see that on the phone bill?"

"Catherine!" It was probably around this time that I began calling my mother Catherine. It was difficult to say "Mom" to someone who behaved in such a stubbornly infantile way. "Why would you let your husband keep you from talking to your mother? What makes you think he'd even want that?" I refused to believe my father would have asked this of her.

Would he?

She sighed and smirked, letting me know I'd never understand what she'd been up against. And to some degree, she was right. This had all taken place in the 1950s. Even beyond the particulars of her Old World upbringing and the corrosive feud between father-in-law and son-in-law, Catherine was saturated with the message that her husband—every husband—needed to be obeyed. Most likely she wasn't the only Fort Benning housewife relying on subterfuge to make it through her day. How many cups of percolator coffee with her new friend before Catherine broke down and asked, "If you'd phone my mom around ten in the morning, my father won't be upstairs, and she can accept the call"?

Clearly my mother wanted me to know how it had been for her as a young wife, and she wanted me to learn a thing or two about my father. Listening, though, what came to mind was my infancy. Before Catherine unloaded her Fort Benning story, I'd done a little reading in psychology, with particular interest in the process by which the self is formed. The infant experiences her mother as, literally, an extension of herself, so every time the mother smiles into the baby's face, the baby gets the message that she is good and her place in the world is secure. If the mother's face reflects anxiety, displeasure, or pain, the infant absorbs the message that she is living in a troubled universe, or that she is troubled, or that she is troubling.

So maybe that's what happened to me. If so, maybe I wasn't a failed adult; maybe I was just someone who—at 2, 3, 5 months old—had spent my days with a mother who was enraged and endlessly anxious about *getting in trouble* if her husband found out she was sneaking phone calls to her mother. When my mother and I arrived at Fort Benning, my parents had been reunited barely one year, after five volatile years of separation. Catherine's father and husband still weren't speaking. She adored both men and was caught between them. How secure could she have felt in her marriage? And would it have been possible for me, as an infant, to feel more secure than my mother did? No wonder I grew up ultra-vigilant to fluctuations in her health and moods. No wonder I so closely monitored my parents, their marriage, our family—not because I was generous-spirited but because of some primal panic about my own well-being. The barnacle's deep concern for the rock.

Oh, for the love of God. Each time I caught myself looking into my babyhood to figure out "what went wrong," I felt foolish.

But maybe it *was* my mother's anxious gaze, or the absence of a peaceful gaze, that branded me with the panic that throughout my adult life has been part of my inner home. Maybe Catherine herself missed out on the prolonged loving gaze when she was born to a teenager. And Gramma Stella? She was born to a mother who'd already lost two babies and had to wonder, *If this new one lives, will we be able to feed her?* Perhaps the anxious gaze is as natural to us as our widow's peak. *Gramma, Mom, I'm no different from you. I'm sad, just like you. I am you.*

That Easter on the beach, learning that my mother spent five years of her young life—*half a decade!*—depressed, enraged by shame, and with no impartial person to listen as she talked through her situation, I thought, *It's a miracle she survived.* How *did* she survive? During those years it would have been virtually impossible for someone like her to find a trained psychologist or counselor, even if she and her family had been able to see beyond the stigma associated with such treatment. In the 1950s, there were psychiatrists and there was in-patient treatment, but there were few options for a person who was distressed while still functioning fairly well.

Somehow, she did survive. She perceived herself as weak, but she was one of the most determined people I've known. For example, she managed to get her marriage back.

But then she wasn't happy with it.

"Mom, why didn't you get divorced during those years, let it go?" Maybe if she could reframe her story, she'd see that, in fact, she had made choices, her fate hadn't been completely imposed upon her. "You were young, Mom. You're attractive. You could've met somebody else." And then I realized that if she had chosen differently, I wouldn't be here, I wouldn't *be*. Once again, there it was, the irrefutable fact that my existence was part of the patch-up of my parents' painful marriage.

"No." She shook her dark head sharply, a gesture that dismissed everything but her peasant fatalism. "There was no way." But I could imagine her with someone different. Maybe a bighearted working man—an electrician or a shop owner, someone who could have given her the financial stability she enjoyed and the medical care she needed. He would have shared the fun times with her, too: bowling leagues, picnics at the Kennywood park pavilions, evenings reclined in twin La-Z-Boys, guessing at *Jeopardy!* I imagined him reaching over to pat her hand when she guessed right, then a fist-pump when his answer was correct. I imagined a man who wasn't always reading medical journals upstairs in his den, but rather could keep his evenings free for TV with his wife.

"No way," she said again, gathering sunscreen, water bottle, getting ready to leave the beach. "It had to be Alfred or nobody." And I realized that for my mother and grandmother and so many women of their times, "the one and only" was not a romantic ideal, it was a mandate: You get one man in your life, that's all. Make the best of it.

Gramma Stella's sewing class in Vazzano. She stands in the 2nd row, to her teacher's right, circa 1920.

Wedding of Stella, 14 ½ years old, and Giuseppe, 28, in Vazzano, December 1929.

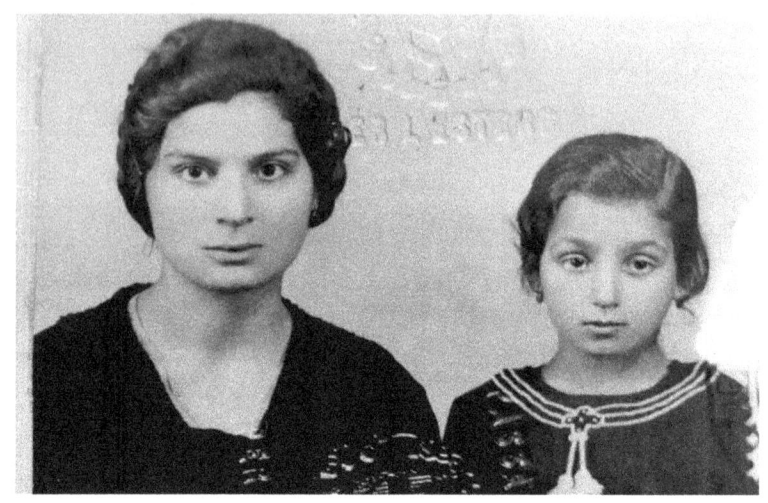

Stella and Caterina's passport photo, spring 1937.

Caterina, now Catherine, 1st grade in Braddock, September 1937.

Alfredo in Naples around the time of his university graduation, July 1945.

Gramma Stella, Catherine, Alfredo, and Grampa Joe in Italy, March 1949.

Catherine and Alfredo in Piazza San Marco, Venice, during honeymoon trip, April 1949.

Catherine sailing back to U.S. from Italy, June 1949.

Catherine and Alfredo's church wedding in Braddock, February 1950.

Catherine visiting Alfredo in Yonkers, September 1950.

Catherine and Gramma Stella, after Catherine and Alfred's reunion, April 1955.

Me with Nonna Anna at her house in Vazzano, autumn 1957.

My brother, Paul, 1 month old, with Catherine and me, January 1960.

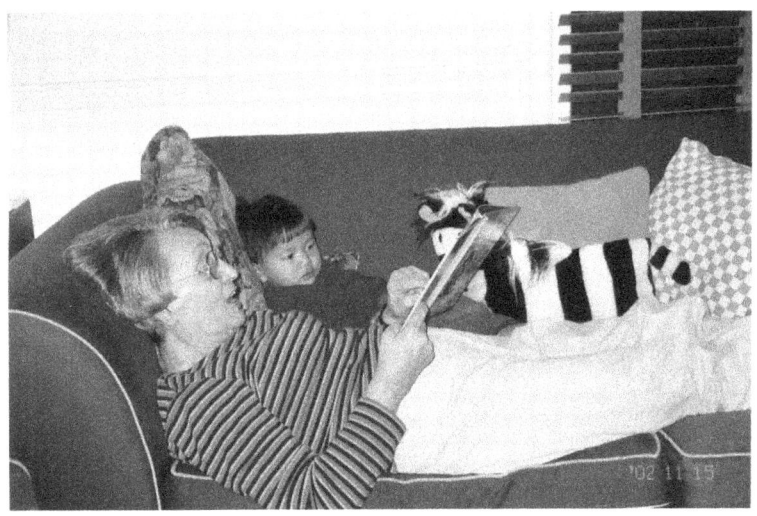

Nonna Catherine reading to Leo, November 2002.
(My favorite photo of her.)

Leo, 10, with Uncle Paul, my brother. October 2010.

Leo, 3, and me, Halloween 2003.

Chapter 10

My Father's Accent

> *Quando il buono non c'è, u triste vale.*
> *When happiness isn't possible, sadness will have to do.*
> —a saying from Vazzano

After my mother's beach talk that Easter, my casual curiosity about my father's immigration narrowed in on one question: Had he really participated in that marriage barter—your doctor-son in exchange for my daughter, who comes with goods (a car?) and U.S. citizenship? Was it possible that my father—my intelligent, high-minded father—had been this calculating in the most important decision of his life? This news simply did not jibe with what I knew of the man.

And I felt, have always felt, I knew my father well. Which is not to say I'm free of the blind spots that afflict most of us when we look at the people we love best. In grade school, a friend told me she liked my father's accent, and I was stunned and said, "He doesn't have an accent."

She laughed. "There's nothing wrong with it, but your dad really has an Italian accent."

After that, I listened for it and even asked him about it.

"Yes," he said, "of course, I have an accent. I was 30 when I learned English." And then I began to hear it. Not much, just enough of an accent to force me to realize that my father had once been one thing—a man completely and fully Italian—and now he was someone else.

In the days following my conversation with my mother, during my frequent beach walks with my father, I considered asking him,

"When you went to Yonkers, was that a marriage separation or was it just for your work?" But I couldn't risk upsetting him. By then, he was weakened by heart disease and asthma. Since childhood, I'd feared my mother's illness; now, I was worried about my father's frailty, too. Besides, if I had asked, he would've changed the subject: "Did you see that pelican? He had *two* fish in his mouth."

My father's delight in the seabirds and the tropical vegetation was genuine. "Look at that!" Seagulls. Parrots. Birds of paradise. Banyan trees. "Look, look." An optimist by nature, he was ready to see beauty when it presented itself. He and my mother were both in the care of the same cardiologist, taking similar meds, waiting for results from the standard tests, but their approach to their respective illnesses could not have been more different. Some differences could be attributed to the fact that the early stages of Catherine's heart disease had been in the 1940s, when there were few remedies and *rest* was the favored medical advice. By the early 1990s, when my father was acclimating to heart disease, *rest* had been replaced by *moderate and appropriate exercise.*

Between Catherine and Alfredo there was also a difference in temperament or, in the parlance of the Ancients, their humors—he, choleric, energized; she, phlegmatic. Catherine organized her day around a few favorite soap operas and talk shows, which she watched while lying on the couch, her arm thrown across her face, the TV rambling on after she'd drifted into one of her many naps. Meanwhile, my father's daily priority was his beach walk, and when I visited, I often joined him.

"This will not be a stroll," he'd remind me as we rode down in the elevator. Once we hit the sand, I had to hustle to keep up. He power-walked to one end of the beach, where he touched the wooden pilings, then turned and headed to the opposite end, where he touched the rocks. "The walk does not count," he'd tell me, mock-serious, "if I forget to touch the rocks." I'd laugh with him, and touch the rocks, too. Occasionally he paused to pick up a shark's tooth (he had a good eye for spotting them) and drop it into my palm. "Here. Don't say I never give you anything." I loved my father's hands.

Out on the beach, we could discuss history, investments, and news articles, and I didn't have to worry that my mother might feel excluded. To describe my talks with my father, I'm tempted to be sentimental—*There were ways I could talk with him that I couldn't with anyone else*—and in part this is true. Mostly, my conversations with him were a relief because he didn't leave me feeling I was supposed to take care of him, save him, the way my mother did.

Even though he didn't invite me to worry—perhaps *because* he didn't?—I was vigilant. Ramping up my anxiety was the fact that though he clearly had his medical situation covered, I was sure his illnesses had a psychological component that he and his doctors were not addressing. For all his intelligence, my father seemed to me stunningly out of touch with his emotions.

For starters, the stress. Years of it, accumulating (though he'd deny it). He was always cheerful after a birth but sometimes didn't sleep several nights in a row because of deliveries. My mother didn't drive, so he was chauffeur for my piano lessons and high-school theater rehearsals, and my brother's athletic events. At home, the tensions were ongoing.

My mother had always had confidantes, and now, in Florida, she also had a therapist, though my father believed that any form of psychotherapy was akin to voodoo. I don't think he talked about his personal life with anyone. The closest he and I ever came to discussing the tensions in their marriage was when I dared to ask, "When you came here from Italy and couldn't find work, did you think about going back?"

"Yes," he said immediately, "I wanted to go. But my mother told me, 'You can't come back here without your wife,' so I stayed."

Nonna Anna was, in her modest way, a maverick, the first in our family to cross the ocean by plane. From her, I never heard the marital gripes that echoed through Gramma Stella's and Mom's stories. When I knew Nonna, she'd been a widow for decades, but her fondness for Nonno Paolo was obvious. She smiled when his name was mentioned. She was a realist, though, not a romantic, with a worldview defined by the exigencies of life in Vazzano, so I could imagine her laying down the law in a letter to Alfredo, telling him, "Not without your wife."

"And Mom wouldn't go live in Italy?" I asked.

"And leave her mother and father?"

With my parents' illnesses progressing, I became more convinced with each visit that if they would see a counselor together and spell out the unholy mess that had started with Yonkers—both of them saying all that needed to be said about the long-ago "arrangements" of their marriage—then perhaps they could get a reprieve from the daily labor of living amid boulders of ancient anger.

One evening I walked into their TV room while my father held the newspaper in front of him and my mother pouted on the couch. The air between them was metallic; there'd been a squabble. Standing under their ceiling fan, I forced myself to speak. "Your anger at each other is making you sick. You need to talk to a third party, and you need to start with whatever happened when Dad went to Yonkers."

I addressed my father: "Mom says you left and didn't want her there."

I addressed my mother: "He says you wouldn't go live with him because you wanted to be with Gramma and Grampa."

To both: "Clearly, you're committed to staying together. That's good, but your history is so complicated. If you could talk this out with someone—not me—you'd be happier. And healthier." *And I wouldn't lose you.*

"In your dreams," my mother said.

"This is not for you to worry," my father told me. "Change the subject."

So I had to drop it. Besides, even though I was convinced that a good, hard, honest discussion would be their salvation—and mine—I was also afraid that their truest emotions, presented outright, might kill them.

A year later, in early spring of 1993, tired of feeling stuck at a plateau, I'd stopped my sessions with Howard and switched to a woman psychiatrist; she, too, harped on separation from family, but she was less kind than Howard had been, so I quit seeing her. Maybe psychotherapy had done all that was possible for me. Maybe it was time to steer my inner life on my own. The publication date for my novel was six months away, and my desk was a happy chaos of catalogs, mailing lists, and publicity—activity that pulled me out into the world. At my new home in Nyack, the landlords' property was bordered by a wall of forsythia. They invited me to help myself, and so I filled my arms with long blades of yellow and stuffed all my vases and jars. When I stepped outside, I could smell the potted sage.

Chapter 11

Urgency

> *and then I took a deep breath, I said*
> *goodbye to my body, goodbye to comfort,*
> *I used my legs and heart as if I would*
> *gladly use them up for this,*
> *to touch him again in this life*
> —"The Race," Sharon Olds

Into the disquieting quiet of my new home, the phone rang. My mother calling from Florida: "Your father's in the cardiac unit. They rushed him there. It's not good." While in the hospital for observation, he'd gone into cardiac arrest.

I did arrive in time. He was going to live. But he had no idea that my mother, brother, and I were there with him in the windowless cardiac-care unit. He was unaware of the resuscitator taped to his mouth, didn't know that his brother, sister, and sister-in-law had rushed from Toronto. This was all before online search engines, so how did we unscramble the information the doctors were pouring on us?

Our father's only chance, they explained, was to implant a fairly new electrical device—a defibrillator. A box the size of a deck of cards would be implanted into his side, just under his skin, and tiny wires would run to his heart to provide a shock when he experienced life-threatening arrhythmias. The surgery couldn't be done in their small hospital, though. We'd have to air-ambulance him across the state to Fort Lauderdale.

And if we didn't opt for the surgery?

The cardiologist was solemn. "His heart is not in good shape."

As we made the flight arrangements, we were still unsure of ourselves, so I was grateful when my uncle said, "I think you and Paul are making the right decision."

Dad was unaware of the plan we were putting in place for him. How thoroughly he belonged to us then. I remember thinking, *What happens to patients who have no one?* I remember worrying about those patients. I remember being afraid that if I didn't shape up soon, I might end up like them—a person who, in an emergency, has no one.

Those days, though difficult, were straightforward. I was a person guided by nothing but love for my father. That's what I remembered. Recently, though, I found a journal entry I wrote during that time:

> I loved my father so fiercely, but in a tortured and conflicted way that tortured us both. This way of love: total preoccupation that excludes so much else, that takes priority over self because somehow this love seems linked to your survival, love laced with anger and the boredom that eventually comes of total absorption. You almost resent this kind of love for all the things it's keeping you from, a powerful love that turns and turns you over, from happy to hateful, filling you and hurting you, bringing you to yourself and stealing you from yourself.

Without this old journal entry, I would have forgotten that Dad's medical emergency was made worse by the tensions between my father and me, my mother and me, my mother and father. Years have passed, and now there is serenity in the way I hold my father in my heart, so the claustrophobia of that journal entry startles me. Of that Fort Lauderdale hospital, I've retained only flash cards of memory. The sun-bright hospital waiting room with thin shades where my mother and I spent slow hours. Each night when we walked out of the hospital, into the merciless humidity, we passed patients in hospital gowns huddled around outdoor ashtrays, smoking cigarettes with one hand and holding onto their IV poles with the other. There it was: the tragedy of how limited we all are in our ability to help anyone, especially ourselves.

*

Dad survived the surgery, the life-saving defibrillator was successfully implanted.

"You just watch," my mother whispered to me in the hallway, "he's going to convince these doctors to send him home, and then what am I supposed to do with him by myself?"

I should move to Florida. She will get sick over this, and it will be my fault.

Against doctors' orders, my father did get himself released, but a few days before he left the hospital, as I fussed around him, adjusting pillows and his water pitcher, he asked me if I had paper and pen because he'd had a dream. "You have to write it down."

He turned onto his side, gazed at the wall, and described a dream in which he was flying over lush green fields. He couldn't emphasize enough how beautiful: "So, so green! Rows and rows of fresh fields." He'd felt happy in the dream—or was it a hallucination?—and he was intent on my getting down every detail. "Write," he commanded. I'll never forget the wonder in his voice: "*Very*, very green!"

It wasn't when the doctor told us, after the surgery, "most likely a few more months, maybe three or four"; it was when I saw Dad's absorption in those green fields he'd flown over in his dream. That's when I got scared. I knew he was leaving us.

As we all knew he would, Dad lived beyond the doctors' three- or four-month prediction, but I couldn't shake the thought, *Where should I be when the next losses come?* Back in Nyack, I'd begun a second novel. With my first one coming out in August, I had the qualifications to apply for full-time teaching jobs. And then I got another unexpected call. No emergency this time, thank God; a heads-up about a one-year sabbatical replacement in an MFA creative-writing program in the Pacific Northwest.

Dream job. I should apply for this. By now, I was 37 and gearing up for what needed to happen next—*baby*. Nearing 40 and still not in a relationship, I'd begun weighing my options to have a child on my own. A full-time college-teaching gig would offer steady income and health insurance. The job would also deliver me to a new place, shake things up. Besides, it was for only one year, and there was always the chance I'd meet somebody out there.

But no! Washington State was almost as far as I could get from the Sarasota Airport—and from my seriously ill father and my struggling mother—and still be in the Continental U.S. *No, I can't do it.*

"Wonderful," my mother said when I told them I'd gotten the offer. "I've always wanted to travel out there."

"Tell them yes," my father said, but I already knew I would.

During this call, I was sitting at my desk in the mudroom of the Nyack garden apartment. It was a wet May evening, and as I looked out the screen door into the rain, I understood that my parents were releasing me into my next life, making it easy for me, asking nothing of me but to do what I'd said I wanted to do: write, teach, live on my own.

In my 20s, I had veered far from my father's vision for me. He'd imagined me as a professional and a mother, living close enough to their house that my family (many children!) could join him and my mother for Sunday dinner. By my late 30s, childless, I'd wandered from my own vision for myself. I may have questioned whether marriage was right for me, but I never doubted that I wanted a child. Now, if I ever did have children, they wouldn't know my father. This grieved me. It's possible I left New York to assure my father before he died that I was at least setting the stage where I'd be ready for his grandbabies when they arrived.

In August, just before I left for Washington, my novel was published, and I visited my parents in Florida and gave a reading in their town library. We celebrated. I returned for Christmas and then again in March, for my spring break, which coincided with Easter. If Dad was strong enough, my parents and I planned to go to Mass on Sunday, but on Good Friday, before dawn, my mother came to my bedroom door and woke me. "He's not good," she said.

I went into their room. He was gasping, sitting up on the edge of the hospital bed. I sat behind him and supported his back, hoping to help him breathe, but, slowly, he instructed me, "Call Lanigan."

The funeral home in Pittsburgh? "No, Dad, no, no." I'm sure I was crying. "It's Easter weekend."

"What better time?" he said.

No, no.

But he knew. Medically, he'd always understood how his illness was progressing.

He died around sunset. We had had the whole day, the hospice nurse giving him morphine, his breathing easing as he slept with the head of the bed angled up almost vertically. The nurse sat on the love seat at the foot of his bed. It was a relief to have someone present who knew what she was doing.

"Tell me about his work," the nurse said, so I did. Later, I realized she probably thought it would reassure Dad to hear my voice. Now and then, his eyes would open and he'd look at us. Three times that day when I sat near him, he lifted my hand and kissed it. I didn't see him kiss my mother's hand. I hope that at some point when I was out of the room, he did reach for her hand, too. Is it too much to hope that she kissed him goodbye?

I must have had a tight mummy wrap on my grief, because eight months passed before I began to unravel. My teaching position had been renewed, so I was living in Washington for a second year. Thanksgiving weekend, the first big holiday with my father gone, had been hard, but I'd spent the day with friends, feeling well surrounded, and I got through it. The Monday after was sunny, very sunny, and as I pulled out of the parking lot of the Department of Motor Vehicles, where I'd just swapped out my New York license plate for Washington plates, a passing car ran into mine. Hard. I was uninjured, thank God, but my poor Honda was nearly totaled.

When I called my mother that evening, I got out the words, "I'm fine, but just so you know, I was in a car accident . . ." and we both started to cry.

I didn't stop crying for months.

I'd been depressed before, I'd been sad, but this was different. By January, I couldn't get close to a full night's sleep. I'd go to bed, fall soundly asleep for a short time, and then be awake for hours. Tiny griefs piled on top of larger ones. *My father will never know my kids. If I ever manage to have kids. It's probably already too late.*

Worries whirled like dervishes through my nights until finally it was dawn and, grateful for the light, I'd latch on: coffee, try to write, read student work, prep classes, teach. I didn't feel like eating much, and then I couldn't eat at all. I was teaching evening classes, and there were a few sessions when the sadness was like fever or arthritis, a physical thing, an ache in my bones, and I had to call a break and go into the ladies' room, stand in a stall, and talk to myself. *You can get to the end of class. One more hour.*

I went to a primary-care doctor, just for a checkup. I don't remember her name, only her kindness. Her hair was long and straight, like Gramma Stella's, so I decided Gramma had led me there. While talking to that doctor, who listened attentively, I realized I was panicking about the first anniversary of my father's death. Relying on the skewed logic of wishful thinking, I'd allowed myself to glide through the aftermath of his funeral believing that while we were still within the calendar year of his death, he wasn't really gone. On a subconscious level, I'd let myself linger in that hammock of time, pretending my father's absence meant only that I had to help my mother with her checkbook and bills, deal with documents and the lawyer, and answer all the thoughtful notes we'd received. *This is just paperwork.* I'd comforted myself with the notion that my father—his spirit—would linger. But by Thanksgiving, the time of the car accident, I had been snatched into the onrush of time: Christmas would be followed by spring, which would lead to the inevitable arrival of the dreaded April 1, the day he died.

"You're depressed," the kind doctor told me and then said what I'd been afraid I'd hear. "I recommend you try an antidepressant, a low dose, so we can see if that helps us get you through this time." Even her word choice was a balm—her *we* and *us*.

But I wasn't a person who needed antidepressants. "I'll exercise more," I promised, "and swim. If I tire myself out, I'm sure I'll sleep better. I'll eat more, too."

Her smile was full of compassion, not a bit of derision, a sad and intelligent smile. "You'll just be a depressed person who's in good shape. Exercise is important, but it won't take care of this."

She did everything right—offered help without forcing it, was low pressure but in no way lax. "It's your decision, of course. If we begin the medication, it'll be a low dose, and I'll want to see you once a week for the first few weeks. I'll need you to check in with me." What convinced me was remembering how much, as a kid, I had wished that penicillin had been available during my mother's childhood illness because it could have prevented her heart disease. Now, the antidepressant. Wouldn't it be wrong not to try?

A few weeks after I began that low dose, I felt the heaviness within me lift. It was early spring in the Inland Northwest. Tiny wildflowers on great slabs of glacier rock. The buoyant air of the nearby desert. These details caught my attention, and sometimes they were so beautiful, I got teary. I still dreaded April 1, but at least I didn't feel alone now. I felt bolstered—by the natural world around me, my friends' voices during long-distance phone calls, books in my hand, good meals at the homes of my new friends. All this had been obscured during my months of depression.

I was still test-driving the antidepressant the last weekend in March, when I headed to Florida. My brother and his family would be there. I couldn't wait to see my young niece and nephew, but I knew that once we were all together, we'd be facing that memorial Mass. The last leg of my trip involved a stop in a minuscule airport somewhere in Florida, where I boarded a toy-size commuter plane. My assigned seat was in an exit row, and my companion was a guy who immediately annoyed me simply because he was there. Buckling my seat belt, I exuded enough chilliness to ward off any small talk, but then the flight attendant appeared to recite the exit-row spiel. "Are you willing to take responsibility?" she asked.

I nodded, and my seatmate grinned and spouted some smart-aleck business about saving himself, and the others can "bloody well figure it out for themselves." In spite of myself, I laughed. His accent was more British than a Brit's (Irish, I learned later), his tone irreverent, his smile savvy and sexy. He was dark-haired, with bright green eyes. A bad boy in a nice sport coat. And fresh, so fresh in every way. He was traveling the world, had been on the road for months. He unloaded all that quickly, not because he was an overbearing talker but because I'd begun asking questions just to hear his voice.

Oh!

I never noticed our takeoff. For the entire flight, my seatmate and I were best friends, confidantes, laughing hyenas. I'm not sure what we laughed about, I only know our conversation was a train that couldn't stop, had no brakes; it was impossible for either of us to say anything that was not clever.

I'm laughing. I can laugh again.

In the back of my mind, I remembered where I was headed and that when I arrived, the next day would be April 1 and my father would be thoroughly gone. But for as long as that plane was in the air, I wasn't the woman I'd been when I boarded.

To exit, we had to stoop as we inched toward the door. Walking behind me, mocking the flight attendants, my friend shifted from brogue to Valleyspeak and whispered, "Buh-bye! Buh-bye!" At this point, anything either of us said cracked us up. We were on the tarmac, catching our breath, waiting to retrieve our stowed luggage. His came first, and he turned to me with an earnestness that was particularly fetching in a guy who had so much of the devil about him. Suddenly he was hugging me goodbye as if we were forever-friends. What a good solid grip of a hug.

"But, wait," I said, not ready for our time to end yet. "What's your name?"

He looked at me. "Damian," he said.

Damian. I never saw the man again, but months later I would come to understand that this had indeed been the devil announcing himself about a week before he actually arrived.

Chapter 12

A Love of the Road

> *Now is my love all ready forth to come.*
> —"Epithalamion," Edmund Spenser

To say that someone is your devil is not necessarily saying he is evil. Not at all. Rather, they can be *devil* as in *dark angel*, the one who will guide you into your dark self.

All the information that preceded my future husband's arrival was cautionary. For spring quarter, he was coming to Washington to work with our students. What I'd heard from the writing community about him: *talented, newly divorced, recovered alcoholic, actually quite brilliant poet, sometimes maybe a little bit out of control.*

My colleagues were overloaded with administrative duties, so I volunteered to show the new guy around. I was a visiting professor with few administrative duties—also I was single with no kids, brokenhearted, and grieving. I had time to help out.

He talked constantly. A talker of the Irish sort, his style long-winded and entertaining. Favorite topic: his recent divorce, his heartless ex-wife, and the myriad ways she'd done him wrong. His divorce was more recent than my father's death, the wound still fresh. He was managing his heartache by traveling, and he'd just returned from an extended stay in Ireland, which was, for him, what Italy is for me—the homeland, an ever-rich source of fascination. From the start, we had this in common. Born in the Midwest, in a working-class neighborhood similar to Braddock, he deeply identified with his Irish heritage.

He hadn't had a drink in over ten years, so he'd keep you up late in coffee shops rather than bars, smoking, talking, talking, then he'd go back to his apartment and write a poem about more of the ways he'd been done wrong. He really was a brilliant poet, at that time experimenting with voices, creating a wide range of personas on the page. The anger was never in his own voice; for himself, he claimed only the incredulity of the tenderhearted victim.

It was interesting to watch, up close, how this poet went about his business. One day he was giving me a ride to campus and he pulled up to a mailbox. He had a fat envelope of poems addressed to his favorite literary journal, but before slipping the packet into the mailbox, he handed it to me and said, "Kiss that for me, will you?"

That spring, I was not at the top of my game, but, on the positive side, during my dark nights of the soul I'd dropped a couple of pounds, which was a confidence booster. A pair of my college jeans fit again. I bought a pair of cute cowboy boots. On that low dose of antidepressant, I was sleeping better; overall, though, I was still just treading water. In the coffee shops, sitting across from the Irish poet, I'd think, *Let him talk. I can stay for another cup of herbal tea, better here than home by myself.* I was sure we had no romantic future—he was recently divorced, significantly older, the father of teenagers, and I was eventually going back to New York.

To keep aloft, I was imposing a strict writing schedule on my mornings, and, while writing, I did not answer the phone. There was a guy in town I always hoped would call me but he rarely did, and another guy I wasn't interested in who called often.

And then, someone began calling daily, mid-morning. They'd listen to my phone-machine message and hang up. The caller's number was blocked, but the insistence of the calls hinted at the poet's style. These interruptions became both a nuisance and a comfort, reminding me of my father's presence—intrusive but also soothing, just like the landscape that surrounded me, visible from every window. Mountains, bulky and roaming, animals of landscape. And against that vast backdrop, my phone ringing. And ringing. It wasn't Sam on the line, and it wasn't my father, and it wasn't anything bringing me closer to *baby*, but it was something.

This visiting guy, this poet, had a new car—two doors, low to the ground—and sometimes he'd call and say, "I'm going for a ride, come with me." I clearly needed to get away from my telephone, so occasionally when the poet called, I'd say, "Why not?"

It was a why-not kind of friendship, nothing advancing it on my side but lethargy. Strapped into his passenger seat, I'd open the window and let all his talk blow right past me. I'd look out at the basalt boulders and pine trees and wonder, *Where is my father now that he's gone?* I'd think about Sam, who, I'd heard, had recently married. I couldn't imagine saying "I do" to anyone other than him, and even with him, my trepidation had won out. How had he managed to say it?

About his own collapsed marriage, the poet maintained that he'd "had no idea anything was wrong." If Gramma Stella had heard this, she would have raised her eyebrows. I cautioned myself: *This poet's a smart guy. Did he really not know his wife was unhappy enough to leave? Is it possible to be in a marriage and not realize it's in deep trouble?* And this had been the poet's *second* marriage. Apparently he was unversed in the deep, probing language of intimacy—all the practices I'd learned about in therapy. Too bad he hadn't been up to the task. Not like I would be—if given a chance.

Occasionally the poet showed me photos of his boys. His love for them was clear and unqualified. Describing the loss of his day-to-day life with his sons, he spoke with raw, unvarnished emotion. Parental love was something I recognized. And because I respected the doting father in him, I let our acquaintanceship slide into a truer friendship.

In late April, I would turn 39, and by now my central preoccupation, besides grief, was my wish for a child. One day, on my back porch, I climbed up onto the slanted roof where the sunbaked shingles felt good if you lay back. I inhaled. Exhaled. In my hand was a thick manila envelope. After making sure no neighbors were watching, I opened the packet and pulled out a long list of anonymous sperm donors. *Age, color of hair and eyes, height, ethnic background.* I was both relieved and aghast that this option was available. All I'd had to do was make a phone call, request an info packet, and it arrived. I read a few pages, then shoved the lists back into the envelope and looked up at the wide sky of eastern Washington. *Has it come to this?*

I mulled over the ironies—I was the daughter of someone who'd delivered hundreds of babies and the granddaughter of a woman who'd had a baby at 15, so wasn't I practically born to give birth? And what about the arsenal of birth control I'd so diligently used? No rewards for responsible behavior? Eventually I climbed down from the roof, onto my porch, tiptoed inside. These lists weren't for me. Not yet.

A nice thing about the poet was that no matter how much I talked about wanting to be a mother, he never made me feel like a walking cliché. With men I dated, I downplayed my baby lust; but with the poet, since romance wasn't an option, I let *baby* become one of our conversational themes, along with Italy and Ireland and his divorce and his kids. One afternoon we were doing errands in Kinko's. "Do me a favor?" I asked him. "See that baby over there? Steal him for me, please."

It was deep spring now in the Pacific Northwest, the air was as clear and blue as a hallucination. In late May, I agreed to a road trip. The poet and I would meet my colleague and her husband in Missoula, Montana. The repairs from the November car accident were finally completed, and this trip would be a good road test.

We were scheduled to leave on Saturday morning, but the afternoon before, the poet showed up at my apartment chatting as happily as usual but looking a bit shy. He'd never come over without calling first, and I'm sure I made it clear I didn't welcome the intrusion. "Well," he explained, "I just had a weird thing happen."

"I'm kind of in a rush," I told him. I was getting ready for a date. I don't remember if it was with the guy I liked more than he liked me or the guy who liked me more than I liked him.

"It's just that I got these odd chest pains this afternoon."

Chest pain? Another one with chest pain? "What are you doing here? You need to call 9-1-1." *I'm supposed to cancel my night out? I'm supposed to take him to the hospital?*

"Actually," he said, "it's kind of going away now."

Looking him over, I was fairly sure the poet was not in medical danger, but how did he know that "chest pain" would get my attention?

With my mother, there had never been a choice; I'd been assigned to her at my birth. But I could still step away from this guy. It would be a bit of a shame, because he was kind of fun, but hey, nip this in the bud.

"Really," he asked, "you think I need to go to the hospital? I don't know."

We're not family, we're barely friends. "I'll call 9-1-1," I said.

"No, no," he said. "Really, I feel better. I didn't want to bother you on the phone."

So you came here in person?

"Either you have pain or you don't," I said, shocked by my own stingy spirit. *But what if his family history is full of heart disease, like my family's?* Still, I held firm, led him to the door. "Call a doctor." When he was safely over my threshold, out in the hallway, I tried to make nice. "Leave me a message later so I know you're all right."

"Okay, and we're still on for Missoula tomorrow."

There's no frigging way. "Let's talk in the morning. I really need to go now."

Looking back, I see that his impromptu visit was one of a few distinct times when I could have stepped away, chosen a path that would have avoided all that followed for the poet and me. I still remember the jolt when he said, "Chest pain." My wisest inner counselor—she often speaks in Gramma Stella's cadences—was on alert, warning me not so much about him but about myself: *You are not the woman for this man.* There probably were women who could get a glimpse of his neediness and not feel their own insides unspooling. Women who could help him without abandoning themselves. But I was not one of those women. *Let this one go.*

And yet that evening, at a movie and then having drinks with my date, I was distracted, wondering if the poet was all right.

The next morning, he called and reported that the ER doctors had given him hearty reassurances. I waited for an opening to beg off the trip. Sipping coffee, wandering my rooms, I must have begun to feel anxious about staying home alone all weekend, because I didn't say no when he said, "So, come on, let's get going. Montana!"

I said, "You're not driving. I'm driving the whole way there and back." He didn't like that. He was used to being pilot, not passenger, but he agreed. So at least I had some control over the immediate situation, and after all, this wasn't my real life. Within a year, I'd be back home in New York. Wouldn't it be crazy to miss the chance to see Montana?

Missoula was our first road trip. The poet surprised me by being a wonderful companion. An hour or so into Idaho *(I'm in Idaho!)* he asked me to pull off the interstate and drive into the hills to an old mission church he knew about. I can't remember the name of it, only that the Native Americans who built the church had decorated the ceiling with the blue juice from local berries. "How did you ever find out about this place?" I asked. I was driving, it was my car, but little by little, I let myself be guided. I was glad I wasn't driving alone when, a few hours in, the Civic got a flat tire. We made it to a roadside garage, where we sat outside on a bench sharing a bottle of root beer—Barq's. The poet took a sip, then tilted his head back and made barking sounds, and when I laughed, he barked some more.

Chapter 13

More Urgency

> *As deep calls out to deep*
> —Psalms 42:7

The poet and I liked to say that before we met, we had been howling our respective pain over distance and time, and we'd heard each other and, finally, come together in the Pacific Northwest. That was one story we told to explain our unlikely union. I was an East Coast woman living an unmarried urban life. He was thirteen years older (just as Grampa Joe had been thirteen years older than Gramma Stella), an accomplished academic and well-published poet who had lived decades of seemingly conventional Midwestern family life—drive the kids to school, mow the lawn. If not for our jobs, our paths never would have intersected, but they did intersect. *Il destino*. Fate.

During our weekend trip to Montana, I felt more open to the poet. We got adjacent motel rooms, and at the end of our first day, after a friendly hug at my door, he went into his room and knocked on our shared wall to say good night.

The next Saturday we drove into Idaho again and wandered through small Western towns. With their worn-down storefronts and faded signs over the doors of old bordellos, they were more like stage sets than actual locales. My life out West often felt illusory and make-believe, a diversion from the real world in which my father was gone.

In late afternoon, we drove to Lake Coeur d'Alene and sat on the beach. We hadn't brought swimsuits, but I felt confident enough with the poet—and flirtatious enough—to crouch down on my beach towel, slip off my jeans and T-shirt, and march down to the shore in my black underwear and tank top. This sounds more scandalous than it actually was—an academic's version of skinny-dipping. I dove in; the water was cold. How long I'd craved this head-to-toe immersion! Swimming out into the center of the lake, I felt cleansed but also greedy, and I dove again. Swam farther. When I looked back to the beach, the poet was watching. By now I liked his eyes on me. I felt not only desired, but also safe. I never would have entered that lake if I'd been alone.

Our classes were over, our grades in. Officially, we weren't colleagues anymore. At the end of that long Saturday outing, while we sat in the car, either he kissed me or I kissed him. Probably it was me. I invited him up to my apartment. After that, he came back every night for two weeks, until it was time for him to drive home to southern Missouri.

Soon we were caught up in a romance so insistent, I delayed my trip to New York City and went to his home for a week in July. When I finally got to New York, the poet and I had such lengthy phone calls that everyone I stayed with was annoyed. In August I returned to the poet's to spend the whole month. The blazing Midwestern heat was the perfect excuse for indulging in a cozy air-conditioned vacation at home.

"Missouri?" my mother asked when I called her. "And what are you doing there, playing house?"

Chapter 14

The Cat

> *It is in the nature of things to be drawn to the very experiences that will spoil our innocence.*
> —*Care of the Soul*, Thomas Moore

One August evening in Missouri, the poet and I were walking down the country roads that flanked his new suburban development, as we often did after dinner. Maybe that evening we were discussing an idea I'd hatched when we'd visited his storage unit. He, too, was a collector of family memorabilia, and while the mementos of his Midwestern childhood were strikingly similar to the stuff in my Nyack storage unit, he outdid me: He had a vintage car—two-toned, with plump fenders. Immediately I concocted a kitsch plan for that old vehicle. We'd park it in his backyard and repurpose it into an outdoor reading nest by reversing the front seat to face the back seat and opening the doors. "It'll be great," I insisted. We could fill the trunk with potted plants. Maybe we were fine-tuning the vintage car idea—we had so many elaborate schemes in those days—while we walked, holding hands and sharing his pipe, until, alongside a cornfield, we came upon a kitten stuck down in a gully.

That's how I remembered the scene, but in an old journal written about a year after that night, I found this:

> We were walking down the country road, it was August, an evening, when, on the brink of an argument, we interrupted ourselves because we heard an insistent crying from the trough of weeds and mud alongside the country road by the chicken farm. We walked over to the sound, happy to be lifted out of our argument, which I had a feeling was

likely to bring us to some irreconcilable place where I'd have to do what I'd been doing with men forever—leave. But instead of having the fight, we found the kitten. The color of her fur sliced her down the middle—half dark, half light. Tortoiseshell patterned, abandoned, maltreated, pulling her wormy butt along the road, crawling with fleas, as small as a hand but as insistent as a fist in the way she socked herself into our lives, into what by then was already the beginning of *our life*. That line down her face always fascinated me. I'd try to touch it, but she'd flinch.

So much for the accuracy of memory. Still, I am certain that while I felt the impulse to jump ship, the poet and I were also making intricate plans for our shared future. Both those things were happening simultaneously that evening when we were hijacked by the cat.

Neither of us wanted it, but we didn't admit that—not to our friends or to each other or to ourselves, not for a long time. At first I wouldn't touch the cat, didn't know what to do with it. I had never cared for anything but a goldfish, though various therapists had told me the unconditional love between pet and owner would be a good lesson in learning to forgive and love myself. But I didn't know where to start. And this wormy, small thing was scarily insistent on getting what she needed, and getting it from us. When we tried to walk away, she twined herself between our ankles.

I kept saying, "We can just keep her in the garage tonight and take her to an animal shelter tomorrow."

He kept saying, "They'll kill her there."

I kept thinking, *So what?* But I didn't say that out loud.

Everything we said skated around the impossibility of making a good choice. We turned and headed home, and the kitten followed, so then she was ours, living on the back patio.

Though the cat helped the poet and me delay our argument, it did catch up with us. By now, our hot points were established:

the many miles between our jobs, and the impossible logistics and economics of our situation. But it was the early days—we'd known each other only four and a half months, had been a couple for only two—and our debates and squabbles almost always unfurled into entertaining duets. Lovers' spats. Foreplay. Usually his dark-blue gaze was provocative.

But one evening during our walk, a quarrel resumed and would not end. Back home, we stood in his bedroom, face-to-face, our bare feet squared off on the wall-to-wall carpet, the air-conditioner venting onto my ankles. I'd never seen him so angry.

"What am I supposed to do?" he was shouting. Just past 50, he still had a young man's compact body generating a nimbus of energy that stirred me; tonight, though, his beautiful hands were fists. The poet never once—not that night or at any point during our time together—touched me in anger, but the volume of his voice now frightened me. Some déjà vu was moving through the room, uncatchable as a bat, flirting from the dark corners and then swooping down, teasing, giving me the creeps.

Twice before I'd participated in shouting matches that felt threatening—once, with a handsome carpenter boyfriend in the hallway of my New York apartment, and then during a brief romance with a volatile peace negotiator in the parking lot of his building. I had immediately turned away from both relationships without a glimpse backwards.

Now, I told myself, *You should leave,* but I stood still.

My sweet-tongued poet had wooed me so insistently that I had flown halfway across the country to be with him, but for this? In my parents' marriage I'd witnessed quiet, corroding sadness, but never this.

"Honey," I tried, "listen, there's nothing between us . . ." How to finish that sentence? *There's nothing between us anymore?* Or *There's nothing between us we can't talk out?* I went with the latter. "Can't we talk?" I whispered. This incited more yelling, and I walked over to the bedroom door to close it. But then, as I turned to face him again, I realized: *No one else is in the house.*

I was scaring myself. My gaze circled his face. Anger had bristled his salt-and-pepper beard. "Just *stop!*" I yelled, curling up my own fists to settle the caffeine-like tremor in my fingers. I was thinking, *It really is time to leave.*

And thinking, *We can't fight like this if we're going to raise kids together.* And thinking, *You're almost 40. What choice do you have?*

And then I cycled around to this: *Poor man is so upset, he needs me, I can help him.* It sickened me to realize that a thrill of familiarity was shimmying up my spine. *I must help* was exactly what had tied me to my mother.

And yet I stayed standing in the poet's bedroom, allowing us to perform several more rounds of useless words. By the time he stormed out of the room, the sun had set, but I didn't turn on lamps. All around me, unformed shadows encroached, whispering, *So this is what you want? This?* I could have left that night, or the next morning, but why fight the ghosts who had finally come to tap me?

Two weeks later, in an act almost as impromptu as our acquisition of the cat, the poet and I married. Just like my mother and her mother, I opted for a marriage of convenience, except I arranged my own betrothal—found the guy myself, negotiated on my own behalf. Like Mom and Gramma, I pledged myself to a man significantly older than I was and whom I'd known less than six months. In the style of my peasant forebears, I collapsed the stages of courtship; I leapfrogged from getting-to-know-you to let's-set-up-housekeeping.

The success of any arranged marriage depends on what happens when the primary parties meet. The poet's teenagers were tremendous. I still remember the thrill when I stood at the front door on Friday afternoons as the younger two arrived for their weekend visits with their dad. Filling my grocery cart with mega-boxes of cereal and bags of chips, I was giddy. *Family.*

There was all this, and more: The poet expressed not one iota of ambivalence about our future. Within a few hours of our ugly fight, we vowed it would never happen again. I decided to let his confidence in *us* assuage my fear. One Monday night after dinner, he proposed.

Of course, I had heard the advice to never marry until you'd been with your partner at least a full year and observed them in every season and during every holiday. Our Memorial Day had been great. Ditto Flag Day. The peasant in me said, *Let's not waste time.* Said, *Do you want to have a baby or not?* Said, *If you marry him, you'll have health insurance.*

This sounds terrible, but it's the truth. I felt I had nothing left to lose.

And as I made my calculations, I was fairly sure the poet was making his, too. His ex-wife had recently remarried. If he married a younger woman, it might make it a bit easier to walk around town. But all that aside, he was a guy who liked being married.

During that August, I learned that it was possible to be calculating and at the same time to fall in love. Who knows, maybe that was exactly what had happened to my parents as they moved toward their own marriage of convenience.

Four days after the poet's proposal, a few hours before our Friday, September 1, wedding, my hair damp from the shower, I slipped on my wedding clothes—a flowered 1940s shirtwaist dress I'd bought two days earlier in a vintage shop for eighteen dollars. None of the standard white froufrou for me. Determined to outwit the marriage demons, I was stripping away everything but the most basic rites.

In my family, everyone married at a church altar, but my ceremony would take place in the poet's home, in the pretty room with a tall window that had recently become my writing room. The poet, with his unfettered enthusiasm, had declared the room mine when I first visited him: "When I bought this house we hadn't met yet, but I knew I was on my way to you, and I wanted this room for you to write in."

I'd never been so avidly romanced. After the drawn-out *maybe* that Sam and I had suffered, I now decided to defer. During the four days before our wedding, the poet did most of the footwork—found the justice of the peace and the jewelry store for our rings. In the tradition of the arranged marriage, I assumed the role of the pliable bride, which actually felt a little bit nice. Something like falling backwards onto a bed of feathers, ignoring that I might sink too deeply to ever lift myself out.

*

But on the day of the ceremony, when the poet ran to the grocery store for flowers, I was suddenly alone in the house and became short of breath. I couldn't stand still with this thing I was about to do. I stepped out into the backyard.

Maybe I'd clip a geranium to put in a vase, maybe cut a tomato from a vine. The next day I planned to make a big dinner for our newly stamped extended family. But then I spotted a mud puddle the sprinkler had left in the dirt yard where the grass hadn't caught on yet, and suddenly, gripped by some primal arousal, I unbuckled my black strappy sandals and sank my bare feet into the mud of rural Missouri. Over and over, my feet lifted and plunged in, insisting on knowing that wet earth, which was as warm as heated towels. *I'm getting married, and this is my peasant pedicure.*

Eventually my heartbeat settled, and I started laughing, as I would have if a troupe of bridesmaids had been with me. And then my closest friends and cousins did surround me; I could almost see them and hear their voices. *An impromptu wedding! This is perfect for you!* So far I'd told practically no one—only my stepsons-to-be, my mother, my brother and his family, who were on their way, knew about the wedding—so in my imagination, my friends could say anything, could convince me, *Yeah, do it!*

I was still laughing when, off to the side, the grandmothers and great-aunts appeared. They'd been hovering since that twilight argument in the bedroom. Bent old village women dressed in their sour black, missing teeth, their twisted braids thinned into *code di lucertole*—lizard tails. If there was a thimbleful of youth left in those women, it was in their eyes, which mocked me. *Silly girl! You think marriage and men can change life into a fairy tale. We were just like you, and now, look.*

As much as those ancient women loved me, they were powerless to divert me on my wedding day; still, they didn't leave without warning, *Bella, you can be married or not, but love will spin you around in ways you can only glimpse while you stand there sunk up to your ankles in the muck.*

Not long after, with my feet rinsed and dried and my sandals buckled back on, I opened the front door and hugged our handful of wedding guests. The justice of the peace was mustachioed and white-suited, and my mother, already thrilled about the wedding, whispered to me, "He looks just like Mark Twain."

By that evening when we all went out to dinner, a man who was practically a stranger was my husband and I was his third wife.

A week after our wedding, I flew back to Washington to start the fall semester. My husband visited a few times over the following weeks. During one visit, I was extraordinarily tired. "Maybe you're pregnant," he said.

I scoffed, but he went out and bought a pregnancy test. The result was positive.

A few days after a doctor confirmed my pregnancy, I sat at a university committee meeting: *I'm sitting at a meeting and I'm pregnant.* Standing at the blackboard: *I'm teaching and I'm pregnant.* At a friend's one evening for dinner, I fell asleep on the couch, and when she woke me and asked, "Are you okay?" I said, "Yeah, just a cold."

I don't know why I told no one I was pregnant.

I do know. *Baby* was too precious a word to breathe into the world. I couldn't risk attracting the attention of the evil eye.

And yet, for all my caution, it happened. I miscarried. Now grief was compounding grief.

After the miscarriage, a surgical procedure, and a subsequent energy-sapping infection, I resigned my teaching position, returned to Missouri, moved into my husband's house full-time. The least I could do was give marriage my best possible shot.

Three months into our cohabitation, I was pregnant again. Optimistic, we brought a videocassette to our first ultrasound to tape the baby's heartbeat.

"What's wrong?" I asked when the doctor and the technician went silent.

The doctor was very young, and so uncomfortable when I started to cry that he said, "Well, you know, you can't really be that upset. At your age, you don't have that many good eggs left," and then he sent in his nurse to schedule the D&C for the next day.

By now, I knew the drill. Before dawn, my husband and I arrived at the outpatient check-in. I hung my clothes in a locker and slipped on the hospital gown, signed forms, lay down on the gurney in my assigned cubicle. One doctor, another doctor, a couple of exceptionally nice nurses dressed in brightly illustrated scrubs that made them look like large children in pajamas. There was an injection. Grogginess. Time passed. An anesthesiologist leaned over me, his cap as tight as a bandage around his forehead, making him look like someone with a severe headache. With soft, fatty fingers, he turned my face toward him. "Can you hear me?" he asked.

"Yes."

"Do you feel that? Do you feel me pinching you?"

I could see his hand on my knee, but, "No, I don't feel anything."

"Okay," the doctor told the nurse, "we're ready."

All day long, at every stage of these quickie surgeries, a capped or masked or unmasked or smiling or worried face suddenly appears over you and asks, "Do you know what procedure you're having done today? Do you know your doctor's name?" These questions are asked a dozen times.

And during the days that followed, I kept asking myself, *Do you know who you are? Do you feel anything?* It was February, but the weather was too mild for winter. The day after the day at the hospital, I walked down our country road. When I got to the narrow overpass that bridged the skinny creek, I stopped and kicked stones into the tiny bit of water below, and that spot—that overpass, that creek—was where my imagination chose to bury the babies, my two invisible babies. In this huge wide world, they, too, needed their place.

As I continued down the road, away from the house—that "the house" was a place I shared daily with another human being was still a jolt to me after having lived alone for so many years—the day was warm, but I was wearing my husband's big sweater, just for the feel of arms around me. The sweater instead of the man. Had I gone for a walk without telling him? Maybe he was working with his door closed again, to keep out the cat.

By this time, she had slashed the window screens, so we'd taken her in for her own surgical procedure. Declawed, unable to defend herself, the cat was now confined to the house. I had named her Gigi, expecting she'd deliver the hard-won happy-ever-after joy of Colette's 1944 novella *Gigi* and the 1958 movie, but no. Sometimes we liked the weight of the cat on us as we lay together on the couch to read. Sometimes we did not. Other times we settled in at our separate desks. I'd pull Gigi onto my lap, and she was a warm heartbeat beneath my hands, but then out of the blue she'd swipe at the keyboard or nip me with her little teeth, and I'd toss her out and close the door behind her.

Just as the poet had promised, the pretty room was now my office, but it was also my refuge, because I had nowhere else to go. For the first time in my adult life, I did not have a job. I had savings, and a little extra had come to me after my father's death, but with no regular paycheck, I was no more successful than my mother had been at "mood management." Vulnerable, edgy. The opposite of what I'd felt when I first arrived here.

Less than a year earlier, when the poet and I were in our sweet, early days of domesticity, my writing room had been tastefully furnished with a formal love seat and an antique secretary desk that had belonged to the poet's mother. In that sun-filled room, I worked on my laptop and had only one small suitcase in the bedroom. If I had left it at that, without returning to my real life to retrieve my worldly goods—including my family keepsakes—maybe our love could have stayed uncomplicated and lovely, as it was during those summer days when I sat at the poet's mother's desk, wondering who she had been, who he was, and what was this new happiness we'd found, which, just like the desk, had all kinds of surprising hidden compartments.

Now, the antique desk no longer fit in the writing room because I'd dragged in my clunky wooden desk, a computer table, several file cabinets, and Gramma Stella's kitchen table and chairs. In the dining room, Gramma's green Hoosier cabinet sat across from my husband's mother's china cabinet, our two beloved family antiques hunkered down in a memorabilia face-off.

We were often in a face-off. Even coming home from the hospital after our second miscarriage, we couldn't manage to stay on the same side. Exasperated by our bad luck and my seemingly endless sorrow, he fumed, "I don't know what to do for you anymore. I feel utterly helpless."

"*You* feel helpless? *You?*"

That night he had his therapy session, which he offered to skip so he could stay home with me, but I urged him to go. When we first met, I was glad he wasn't closed off to therapy as my father had been. But the night of our second miscarriage, he came home from his session with a sleeping-pill prescription that his doctor had written—*for me*. Though this psychiatrist—I think of him as Dr. X.—knew nothing about my medical or psychological history, didn't know if I had allergies or an addiction, didn't know a thing about me, he'd prescribed pills for me.

"He could lose his license for this," I told my husband.

"He's trying to help you! The man knew you'd be upset, and he went out of his way to make sure you could at least sleep. He's being *kind*, and you want his license."

"You really don't see," I whispered, "that what he did was wrong?" It was a hall-of-mirrors moment. I was trying to have a child with a man whose judgment seemed to me utterly skewed. "You're kidding me, aren't you?" *Please tell me you're kidding.*

No kidding.

Two nights later, still devastated by loss and my chaotic hormones, confused by my husband's allegiance to the pill-dispensing psychiatrist, fuming, I went into my office and sat with my feet up, but then I realized there was no reason to pamper my body. The baby was gone. I stood and pulled the heaviest boxes of books down from the closet shelves and hauled them out to the garage, where I dug into my storage. Turning anger into muscle, engaging the abdominals I'd allowed to turn to mush below layers of early-pregnancy fat, I tilted boxes onto their sides and began eviscerating them. All sentimental excess had to go. I tossed books, journals, and love letters across the garage into the trash bin. I threw in sweaters and stuffed manila folders. If I was being stripped of my future as a mother, I was going to purge my past, too. My husband, wisely, kept his distance.

Hours later, when I entered the kitchen, I couldn't look him in the eyes. I was as committed to my anger as I'd ever been to anything, but he hugged me. Exhausted, trembling, I held my fists against his shoulders, cried, and admitted, "I don't know any other way to be. I'm sorry I'm so sad."

He held me a long time and eventually got me to laugh, telling me, "You cry yourself to sleep every night. I think that going to bed makes you sad." Then, softly, he admitted that sometimes when I cried really hard, he felt envious. I appreciated his trying to help me save face.

The next day he offered, "A drive in the country?"

"Perfect." I made a pact with myself: I would not allow the words *baby* or *Dr. X.* or *divorce* into my thoughts, and eventually I was soothed by our long, quiet ride. When we got home, though, we found that Gigi had spent her day attacking a roast beef thawing on the kitchen counter.

"Did you leave that roast out?"

"Why would I leave that out?"

"But I hate roast beef!"

We had no right to be upset. Gigi's patterns, by now, were clear. For a day or two, she would do no harm. Then, predictably, she'd do something unpredictable and destructive. Some mornings we'd find our framed art work askew because Gigi had literally climbed the walls. We wanted to trust her, but too often we were woken by the sound of something breaking on the kitchen counter in the night, and then I'd have to face the fact that an animal really did walk on the surfaces where we prepared our food.

"Maybe you're not cat people," a friend suggested, "or maybe she's not your cat."

My growing fear was that Gigi very much was our cat: unpredictable, sniping, beautiful, Janus-faced, affectionate, and increasingly dark.

I had no right to be shocked by what went on between the poet and me in marriage. I was too old to be naive about the discord possible between two people who'd pledged to love each other forever even though their previous pledges had not gone well. There were moments when my love for my husband was richer than what I'd felt for any guy before. He was my husband, I was his wife, and I discovered, to my surprise, that the marriage bond did make a difference. When we were with his children, I had a sense of *home* as powerful as any I'd wished for. Yet, as good as the poet and I often were together, we were eventually brought down by a meltdown—sometimes his, sometimes mine—that was a variation of that explosive August night before we married.

"Who are we," I asked him once, "when we get the way we do?"

"Two people," he said, "who are frightened."

Occasionally, I understood it was my own anger I feared.

That summer, I visited friends in New York for a few days, and while I was there, my husband called to tell me he'd put an ad in the local paper, and a mother and her daughters had just come to our house and taken Gigi away.

"You gave her away without asking me first?" I tried to sound upset, just as in the early days I'd tried to pose as a person who liked cats—*Here, kittykittykitty.*

"Sweetheart," he said, "you don't want that cat under our feet any more than I do. We tried, and it didn't work."

I had to concede he was right. I admitted that I, too, was sort of relieved to be rid of her. I bet we even laughed together. But later, after we hung up, when I was alone, I couldn't help wondering what, exactly, we'd given up on when we gave away that cat.

Chapter 15

Caesura

> *The purpose of using a caesura [in a poem] is to create a dramatic pause, which has a strong impact.*
> —Literary Devices website

I lived in the house in Missouri for one full year. Of my hundreds of nights there, I remember warm Sunday evenings when, after our walk or a drive into town for dessert, I'd linger in the driveway and look at our country sky patched up with stars. Summer nights cluttered with insect noise and the slanting scent of chicken shit had an end-of-the-world texture to them.

You wanted to reinvent marriage, and here's what you came up with.

On good nights, this thought made me smile. I was now a sandal-footed, dusty woman who lived near pastures and wore all manner of thrown-together clothing, hair pulled up into odd piles. As a married woman in Missouri, I felt more solidly on latitude with Vazzano, my family's village, than with New York or Washington or any life of my own imagining, and I'd willingly brought myself here. *What am I meant to learn?*

I had so harshly judged my parents and grandparents for their inability to be happier in marriage. It shamed me now to remember I used to challenge my mother and grandmother: *Why don't you just leave him?* But back then, I knew nothing about the way troubles in marriage move like water—ever shifting—and it's often not clear if you're swimming or drowning. You can't know this until you're navigating the rapids of your own married life. Every time my husband and I floated into peaceful waters, I believed fully in our marriage. And when the undertow caught us, I hated myself for my inability to either improve the marriage or decisively end it. All my therapy and insights, for what? Mostly, I wondered how anyone could work at marriage as hard as I did and still be so bad at it.

How modest our wedding had been, with a slight air of desperation to it, like the wartime weddings I'd heard about in Italy. One of my uncles had had a friend whose wedding shirt had been quickly sewn from the cloth of an American soldier's parachute.

I'd parachuted myself into marriage as if on a mission, its purpose urgent but unclear, landing myself in a place both mysterious and hauntingly familiar. On those nights of intermittent grace, when the country stars hung over our house just so, I felt proud of my husband and myself, engaged, as it seemed we were, in a noble experiment in the redemptive powers of middle-age love. It's important for me to remember that our marriage included these times, too.

I booked a room in a church where I led private weekly writing workshops, which gave me the chance to leave my cramped office and spend time with people. I met good people, and making a little money brought me closer to a way of life I recognized. But it wasn't much money. Since I was 21, I'd had steady income. I still had savings, but by fall, they were dwindling, as was my sense of independence. So when I got an invitation to teach an eight-week course in New York the following winter, I said yes.

Yes Yes Yes.

Emboldened by that offer, I made phone calls, mailed letters, and put together a few other gigs. January through March, my husband and I would commute between Missouri and New York City. Lucky for me, my subletter in the city was ready to move out of my apartment, so I was able to step back into my former life. More or less.

That was what I told people. The truth: I hadn't left Missouri because I had jobs in New York. I'd set up those jobs so I could leave Missouri. So I could get some distance from my husband.

We were separated.

I didn't use those words—not when I spoke to others or even to myself. *We're working on things*, I told my closest friends; and they kindly repeated, *Yes, you're working things out*. I'd left the house in Missouri on December 4, one year and three months after our wedding and exactly one year after I'd moved in. My New York jobs weren't scheduled to begin until mid-January, but during Thanksgiving weekend, our arguments had crescendoed, and this time when I reached my limit—*Should I book a hotel room? How soon can I get to the bank?*—I didn't talk myself down. Instead, I closed my office door, got on the phone, and, in a lowered voice, reserved a U-Haul truck. The phone number was handy. I'd weighed the U-Haul option before.

What happened over Thanksgiving weekend was that I gave an ultimatum: My husband had to stop seeing his psychiatrist, Dr. X., or I'd leave.

If someone had ever intruded on my therapy in that way, I'd have been furious. But my husband often returned from his sessions more volatile than serene. These observations were minor red flags, except, when coupled with the sleeping-pill prescription, they added to my concerns about Dr. X. In August, nearing our first anniversary, I felt so much disequilibrium in our home, I packed a bag and called my husband from town to tell him I was headed to the airport. After we talked for two hours on a pay phone, he said he'd stop seeing Dr. X., not because he agreed with me but because I'd asked him to.

"Thank you," I told him. "It means a lot to me that you're doing this for me. And for our marriage."

Autumn passed calmly enough. By then, I was seeing a new therapist, someone I'd connected with from the start. For one thing, she agreed with me that Dr. X. shouldn't have prescribed sleeping pills for me, which helped me feel safe with her. Whenever I was in a panic about my marriage, she'd tell me, calmly, "Respect the force that drew you to your husband."

But then, one afternoon in late November, I sat down at the dining table to open the mail, and on the monthly health-insurance statement I learned that my husband had never stopped his sessions with

Dr. X. That night at dinner, he made it clear he intended to continue seeing him. Thanksgiving weekend, with company in the house, we avoided each other. Sunday night, I told him, "It's either him or me."

The next day, I had to wait until my husband left for class, and then it was a race against time to figure out what to pack. Filling suitcases and boxes, I was in constant conversation with Gramma Stella, my mother and her cousins, Aunt Mamie, all the women who'd raised me.

As I imagined them sitting around a coffee cake from our favorite Braddock bakery, I distinctly heard their voices reminding me, *Grab a couple towels. And blankets. Just hurry!* My plan was to have the truck loaded by the time my husband got home, and then I'd tell him I was leaving now rather than in January.

Or should I leave before he gets home and call him from the road?

I wasn't sure yet, but I was relying on those women huddled just above me, their voices from Braddock offering their best wisdom.

What's she waiting for? She should leave now, *before he gets home.* Some were timid in marriage, like my mother.

No! She needs to talk to him, he's her husband. How would that be, him coming home and her gone? No! Others had companionable marriages and were willing to give a guy the benefit of the doubt.

And if he gets angry? You wouldn't catch me *staying there, knowing how he gets.*

But she loves him.

Yeah, well, she'll get over it. Everybody does.

Their voices were jumbled, so I was uncertain who was urging what, I just knew that, together, they were covering all the bases. *Don't forget the colander!*

But he'll need the colander!

Too bad for him. She needs it, too. Besides, how long before he has somebody else in there cooking for him, some other little dummy?

Hey, she's no dummy. She just needs to rush and get out of that house.

Don't worry, dear, it's all in God's hands—this could only be Gramma's voice, no one else's. *We don't know the future. But yes, you made this decision to go, so now you better hurry up.*

*

When he got home, my husband was surprised to see the U-Haul with my car attached to the back and to hear my news, but he stayed calm, and I was grateful for that. As we talked, the phone in my office rang twice—I had asked a friend and my brother to check on me around seven-thirty, when I knew my husband would be back home, in case we argued, in case the arguments got worse than ever.

None of that happened. Instead, he prepared a nice dinner for us.

I don't remember if we made love that night or not, but I do know the mood was such that we might have, as strange as it seems. I do remember that we lay on the futon reading, our night-table lights on, our feet touching, commenting on how "not uncomfortable" the futon was—the mattress and box spring I'd brought to the marriage were now loaded onto the truck, thanks to the help of a teenager I'd hired. As my husband and I held hands, I hoped that, with some work, we could not only return to this blessedness but even figure out how to live this way permanently.

The next morning, as we said goodbye at the front door, I was the one who raised my voice. "I don't want to be leaving here. This is our home." He hugged me a long time. Crying, I climbed into the truck's cab and drove slowly through the streets of our development and out onto our country road, past the grazing cows and the collapsed barn that had been a destination for our evening walks. I made a left turn onto the two-lane. When I finally reached New York, about a week later—I'd spent a few days with my cousins in Pittsburgh—all I had to worry about was what I should do next.

Chapter 16

The House

> *It is easy to see the beginnings of
> things, and harder to see the ends.*
> —"Goodbye to All That," Joan Didion

The salve of city life no longer worked for me when I drove back to New York. I was a ghost in my old life. Or I was living with the ghost of my former self. The teal-blue push-button telephone still squatted on the hallway table, but for talking to whom? A different *me* had lived here—as a daughter, as Sam's girlfriend, as a *Time* copy editor, as a patient of Howard's. Now I was a part-time instructor, a novelist whose one book was out of print and whose second novel was barely crawling along. I was a poet's wife, pledged to a marriage I had to distance myself from. I wasn't anyone's mother, though I was a stepmother, and my stepsons were boys I loved with enormous affection. But those boys already had an excellent mother. They accepted me graciously as their father's partner, but they needed my mothering much less than I had a need to mother.

Mother mother mother.

When and how and would I ever have a child? Daily, I was moving closer to my 41st birthday. What was I going to do about that?

My greatest solace that cold December in New York came from telephone sessions with my therapist in Missouri. Ten months earlier, at our first sessions, I'd been determined to make a yes-or-no decision about my marriage, but she wouldn't help me with that. "The best thing you can do for your marriage," she insisted, "is to pay attention to yourself. You've lived your life taking care of your sick mother and worrying about your parents' marriage and everybody else, so now—"

"Yes, but how do I tell my husband—"

"We're not here to talk about him. You can't change other people. You're not that powerful."

My work with Howard had been largely focused on *father*. This new psychologist was the first to direct me toward *mother*. All my life I'd done comic riffs on my mother, her neediness and our bickering, but to sit still in therapy and actually *feel* how it was to be her daughter—that made me squirm. For starters, she had, in many ways, done everything right. Three good meals on the table daily. Pantry full of treats. I had never lacked for clothes or thoughtful gifts or elaborate birthday parties. More important, I had gone out into the world knowing my mother loved me. Still, it was becoming increasingly apparent that my reserves of self-regard and self-care were piddling. My new therapist was suggesting I didn't have to go through my days feeling so depleted.

This was news.

Yet every time she asked me, "What can you do to start taking care of yourself?" I felt I was being handed an empty bucket.

I was only beginning to see how close I was to my mother, and always had been, but it was a closeness that tied me to her frailty. Love, for me, was that body of hers, within which anything could go wrong at any moment. *Mom, do you have chest pain? Are you still dizzy?* In my adult life, any romance—offering, as it did, physical intimacy—returned me to that tenuous, nerve-racking closeness I needed to protect myself from.

"Okay, okay, I see," I conceded. "But how do I change this?" I asked my new therapist.

"You sit with it."

One of her most effective tools for modeling her message of self-care was a cashmere throw draped over the ottoman of her upholstered chair. Occasionally she'd pull the cashmere up over her arms. I don't remember her lifting her feet onto the ottoman, but it was there, suggesting the deep comfort of curling up with a book and letting the world go by.

Dr. Cashmere.

In December, in addition to "start taking care of yourself," she introduced another theme to our phone sessions: "You're dealing with your husband's untreated alcoholism. I think you'd find support if you went to Al-Anon meetings."

On his behalf, I was offended. "My husband *does not drink*. He hasn't had a drink in over a decade. I don't doubt his sobriety at all."

"This isn't about drinking," she explained. "In the absence of alcohol, there can still be alcoholic behavior. It's a syndrome. There's even a name for it: dry drunk syndrome. You can read about it."

Was this syndrome real? Was this what was happening in our house? Occasionally, when my husband was in a difficult conversation and there was an unexpected shift in the topic—"a sideswipe"—he'd become outraged. My earnest, though probably misguided, solution was to try to talk the problem out, but then he'd clutch his hair with his fists and storm out of the house. Those abrupt exits terrified me, but I was also pissed off by the drama, which seemed, at least in part, staged to keep me at a distance. *Is he pulling this shit to scare me?*

Or did I need to be more compassionate? This dry drunk syndrome, if it existed, sounded as mysterious as miscarriage—another family affliction that was invisible yet painful and insidious.

"He might change his behavior," Dr. Cashmere told me, "but you can't change it for him. The best thing you can do for yourself, for your husband, and for your marriage is to go to Al-Anon."

I had just left my husband and was desperate to figure out *a plan*. I told Dr. Cashmere, as politely as I could, that she was wrong.

Besides, during the long phone conversations my husband and I had most nights, his voice was particularly somber as he told me, "There are things to work out. I want to do that." Most effective was his usual sign-off: "If you're leaving, take me with you."

Christmas Day, I spent alone. I could have been in Atlanta, at my brother and sister-in-law's, where my mother was visiting, but I didn't have the energy to travel. I had planned to go to a friend's for Christmas dinner, but the night before, she called to let me know her children had contracted head lice at school. She knew I couldn't risk it. Right after Christmas, I'd be taking the train to Washington, DC, for the Modern Language Association conference, where I had seven interviews lined up for university teaching jobs. I couldn't go down there scratching my head.

As far as I knew, no one in my immediate family had ever spent Christmas alone. *Howard, is this the separation you were talking about?* Even during the years my father worked in different cities, making little money and separated from my mother, he had found a way to get to Toronto for the holiday. His youngest brother had immigrated there with a few other young men from Vazzano. They shared one room and had a hot plate to boil their pots of pasta. For Christmas, Dad made sure he got up there to join them.

It was simply wrong to be alone for the holiday. But—and this was surprising—I wasn't miserable. Practicing what Dr. Cashmere had taught me, I checked in with myself: *Do you feel safe here by yourself?* Yes. *What can you do to help yourself?*

I'd bought a small box of Godiva chocolates on Columbus Avenue, and that gold box on my kitchen counter was a treat but also a reminder that though this Christmas Day was paltry compared to my family's traditional feast, I was blessed in a million ways.

Are you practicing gratitude? Round the clock.

How is your serenity? Not bad. *And your energy?* I'm preserving it.

The trip to DC would be my chance to resuscitate my teaching career, which I'd abandoned when my first miscarriage derailed me. As I tried on my interview clothes, I prepared for the questions I anticipated: *Please discuss your teaching philosophy. What are your strengths as a teacher? And now tell us what's up with all this moving around—Washington? Missouri? New York? What's your deal, lady?* On Boxing Day, at Ann Taylor, I found a deeply discounted black silk turtleneck—perfect under my interview jacket—and decided to interpret this sartorial find as a good sign. For better or worse, I was ready.

After the conference, in time for New Year's Eve, I visited my husband in Missouri, where he helped me practice my presentations. I was still in the running for three of those seven jobs.

In April, I got an offer from the University of Nebraska at Omaha, a seven-hour drive from our home in Missouri. Doable for a commuter marriage. On the weekends when the kids were with him, I would drive to Missouri; the alternate weekends, he would drive up to me.

Traveling back and forth between our two homes, I felt my life was double full. When it was my husband's turn to drive, he'd call from a gas station in Maryville to report the price of gas, and I'd know he was two hours away. Maryville stations had the best prices on our route—sometimes less than a dollar a gallon—and we savored that nice bonus tucked into our travels. We really were trying to make the best of things. Later, when I heard his footsteps cross the wooden floor of my front porch, I'd push my schoolwork aside and rush into the first hug of the weekend. Weren't we clever to have arranged our marriage as a series of recurring honeymoons?

And yet, after a day's drive, and homecoming sex, and dinner, and unloading the luggage—which included the ever-present stack of student papers, along with our own manuscripts to work on at some point during the weekend—the driver was always tired. One or the other of us usually had trouble getting to sleep. Some weekends, I was measuring my temperature to chart my ovulation. Messing with progesterone treatments. I remember taking a pregnancy test in the restroom of a gas station in Benton, Missouri. It came up negative, and my crying jag added an extra hour to the drive.

Maybe once we have a baby, we'll be fine. Sometimes I believed that. Other times, we argued in that way that obliterated all the good between us. *I'd never bring a child into this.* Pulling into the driveway, I'd look at our windows and wonder, *What will happen in there this weekend?* The house seemed to stoop, weary of our moods.

And then one Sunday in spring, I was driving back to Omaha through a heavy, boring rainstorm. I don't remember if that weekend's visit had been good or turbulent— usually they were both. What I do remember is sitting in slow-moving traffic, already sick of my music tapes, so, in my imagination, I wandered into the rooms of a house for sale in Omaha that I'd recently looked at for the second time.

My job was going well, so it didn't make sense to keep doling out rent. Unlike Gramma Stella, who had had to hand over her earnings to Grampa, I had the chance to make a long-range investment. My husband and I could have a two-house marriage.

The bungalow I'd found in Omaha was three minutes from campus and a block from where I was renting, in a neighborhood that was a wonderland for someone from New York. On the street corners, instead of overflowing trash cans, there were landscaped triangles of rosebushes, hostas, or other perennials that someone took time to water and weed. Flowerpots hung from streetlamps. This was Omaha's Midtown, an urban residential area that, to people who favored the new suburbs, seemed not only unsafe—occasional car break-ins and other city nuisances—but also inconvenient, because the garages were small and the old houses had tiny closets. The Midtown sidewalks were cracked, and heavy limbs of ancient trees hung in arches that surrounded you as you wandered from block to block. I wandered a lot when I wasn't working. I didn't have close friends yet in Omaha, and, walking at twilight, I was particularly aware of living in a world that no longer included my father. Those streets became my companions, offering up small but reliable solace, continuous pleasure for the eye.

That low rock wall at the brick house with persimmon shutters. The colonial with the worn chimney climbing up against the flat, wide sky. Curved cement benches atop berms of intricate greenery. I hadn't fallen for a neighborhood in this way since I'd lived in Rome and been hypnotized by the terraces, balconies, and ancient tiled entryways. In Omaha, it was blooming window boxes, Art Deco moldings. No two houses were alike. Craftsman, Prairie style, Queen Anne, Spanish stucco, tall houses and squat ones, apartments and mansions. The neighborhood was egalitarian. Next door to the cottage I had my eye on was a duplex rental; three blocks away lived zillionaire Warren Buffett. And in this neighborhood—better than in Rome or New York—a house, a *whole* house, was possibly affordable. Still, I was intimidated by the prospect of taking such a serious step, terrified of the way it would tie me down to the Midwest, so far from home, wherever that was. At the same time, I was weak-kneed with house lust.

Gabled roofs, bay windows, porch swings.

It wasn't eye candy; it was bread, sustenance. I walked those streets in the darkening evenings of my first autumn in Omaha and trudged through snow in late-winter afternoons. Here, I thought, the domestic gentleness I long for can be obtained.

The house of my daydream as I drove from Missouri was a pretty cottage with problems. A few friends had walked through it with me and pointed out that the master bedroom had neither heat vents nor a closet; nonetheless, I was smitten. Who needed vents and closets when your bedroom had five huge windows, letting in heaps of light and a view of neighborhood treetops?

I loved that the house followed no standard floor plan, for within it I would live no standard life. The central room was over a hundred years old, and various rooms jutted off it. One was big enough for a piano and not much else, another had space for bookcases and could be a perfect office. The galley kitchen had a sliding glass door, which would be convenient to crack open while I prepared holiday banquets. I'd invite everyone—friends and family from New York, Italy, Pittsburgh, Atlanta, Canada, Missouri, Washington. With I-80 just four miles away, guests could arrive easily. The dining area wasn't large, but the place settings at Gramma Stella's green table would, like the fishes and loaves, magically accommodate all of us.

Upstairs, the attic had been punched out to create an A-frame loft where I could set up Gramma's sewing machine and a rack for my collection of dresses, coats, and gowns she'd made. There was room under the skylight for a reading chair. And when my child arrived, however he or she arrived, we'd cuddle as our books piled up all around us.

From my first fantasies of that house, a child lived with me there, enjoying a perfect childhood. I wasn't a mother, so I felt confident I knew exactly how a child should be raised. A small house with good light and books everywhere. Construction paper, clay, yarn, colored pencils available always. Little or no television, lots of music. I still had my turntable, so my child would learn the basics straight from LPs. Beatles, Bruce, Bach, Vivaldi, and jazz. Lots of jazz, especially Brazilian. We'd samba through the rooms, each one painted a different color: coral, vermillion, aqua, periwinkle, and other rich colors with beautiful names. And how convenient that the washer and dryer were right around the corner from the kitchen. I could do laundry as soup simmered, while my child and I skidded in our socks up and down the long linoleum kitchen floor. We'd make a game of vacuuming—*vroom, vroom!*—to reinforce the idea that everyone in the household—all two of us!—pitched in on chores. The floors would always be clean, as would the bathtub, where my child would soak in bubbles as we sang and played with plastic bottles and jugs. Expensive toys would not be necessary.

Most important, in the house where my child would grow up, there would be no dust bunnies of anger in the corners, no cobwebs of words tangling us up, no fine film of sadness as relentless as dust on the woodwork. My vision of perfect mothering, like a massive spring-cleaning, would establish a new order. That I might best accomplish this vision as a *single* mother was an idea I was still trying to squelch; but one thing was decided: I could find no better staging ground for my child's ideal childhood than that funky Omaha cottage. It would be the manifestation of the old saying "Safe as houses."

At the end of that rainy Sunday drive, when I turned to look into the Civic's back seat, it was a shock, and a disappointment, that there wasn't a child back there strapped into a car seat. Not yet.

Something dangerous was happening to my marriage. My extended fantasy of raising a child—and doing it alone—gripped me so powerfully, it was like falling in love. Turning away from this desire was not possible.

But I second-guessed myself a lot. *Have a baby and raise it alone? And with what money? And when you work, who would take care of that baby? No!*

Still, I went to look at that little cottage several more times.

*

Over the following months, on every page of my journal, I recorded an endless loop of indecision. I called a lawyer in Missouri and another in Omaha to discuss the fine points of divorce versus legal separation, telling them repeatedly, "This is just research."

My mother had no patience with my doubt. "Yes, you should get divorced. What are you waiting for?" During her one visit to our home, she'd heard my husband and me arguing in our bedroom, and later, as I drove her to the airport, she said, "I'm sorry, but I'm not coming back here. I lived with that for years, and I'm done with it. If you want to live that way, it's your business." Though she enjoyed the poet's humor, her early enthusiasm for our marriage had faded.

During one of our phone calls, I asked her, "Why didn't *you* get divorced? Like, that time you dragged us down to Gramma's while Dad was away. What happened?"

I expected she would put me off as she had in the past, but this time she answered me. "How could I get divorced? He was a doctor, he'd get big lawyers. I had no way to keep him from taking you kids away."

If I got divorced, would it be because my mother hadn't been able to?

Meanwhile, my baby's spirit hovered somewhere in the universe—I felt that. I made an unyielding promise that when the child arrived, there'd be no raging within our walls. Anything counter to the health of body, mind, and soul would not be allowed. *Healthy. Boundaries.* These words were my new mantras.

"Exactly," Dr. Cashmere told me. We were still working together over the phone, but by now I was also, once or twice weekly, attending Al-Anon meetings. She had finally broken me down.

No, that's not true. By midwinter of my first year in Omaha, my own inner life had broken me down.

Like so many others, I went to Al-Anon ready to vent about my spouse, and I'm sure I did. But what I learned, as many do, was that I'd needed Al-Anon and its message of self-care long before I met my husband. It was the standard family-of-origin thing: In my marriage, as in other significant relationships, I had, uncannily, either sought out or re-created the same unsatisfying role I'd performed in childhood. More than figuring out the fluctuations in my marriage, I needed to address the seemingly irresolvable triangle of mother–father–me. None of this was news, but those meetings, with their optional one-dollar donation, cut to the chase in a way that psychotherapy, which had different goals, did not.

One winter night at a meeting, I listened as a woman talked about how surprised she'd been to learn that her husband was an alcoholic. "In my family," she said, "we were teetotalers." As I drove home, *teetotaler* stayed with me, and suddenly I was thinking about Grampa Joe. Sitting at a red light, I remembered that Grampa never raised a glass, not at holidays, weddings, or family dinners. "When I was young, drinking made me crazy," he told us when we were kids, "so no more." *Teetotaler*.

The next night, I was on the phone with my mother and a curious question came to me. "Mom, do you think Grampa was an alcoholic?"

"Pfff, *no!*" She laughed. "He wasn't an alcoholic." Slight pause. "But the drinking. Ha! I'll tell you. In the old days, sure, he'd be downstairs in the bar with the men and playing cards, and sometimes he'd have a little too much, they all would, but that was nothing. But then, those years when all that mess was going on, oh, boy."

"When you and Dad were separated?"

"Yeah"—her voice flat—"those years. After your father left, your grandfather was fit to be tied. He'd get so drunk and then come upstairs and scream at your grandmother, 'You see what you did! This is your fault.'" My mother's voice had amusement in it, as if this were a crazy reminiscence you just had to shake your head at. "He'd yell and grab her by the hair and pull her down those steps. Yeah, it was not good."

"What?" I stood up from the couch, all fight-or-flight. "He pulled her hair?"

"I'm telling you. Down those steps, he'd pull her. He hit her. You don't know the half of it. One time he showed up with a gun, and he's slamming that gun on the table."

"A gun?"

"Slammed it right down on that green kitchen table you have. He's pounding and yelling, 'I'm going to kill him.'"

"Kill who?"

"Your father, that's who. 'If he shows up here again, I'm going to kill him.'"

I stared at the table across the room. Gramma's kitchen set with its six solid chairs, where she had sat and shared confidences with her friends, where she had spread out sewing patterns and kneaded the weekly bread. When I'd packed up that furniture to move it to New York, my father had told me, "It's old! Toss it!" *Never.* From New York to Washington to Missouri to New York again and then to Nebraska, that table was the centerpiece of my home.

As Mom went on—"Those days, I'm telling you. . ."—a memory came to me from the afternoon of Grampa's funeral, when one of the cousins reminisced about helping Grampa down at the bar. "So there was a law," my cousin said, "that you had to break the empty liquor bottles. They didn't want you refilling them with liquor you made yourself, so Uncle Joe, he'd go downstairs and take off his good shirt. He'd be in his undershirt way down in that basement room, the one with the dirt floor, and he'd throw those empty bottles against the stone wall. Smash 'em."

It was unsettling, in the solemnity of his funeral day, to have my mild grampa brought up before me as a man wearing a wifebeater, hunkered down in that dark cellar, smashing liquor bottles, slivers of glass skittering across the floor. Now, in my mother's story, that version of my grandfather reappeared. *A gun?*

"What do you think Grampa would have done if Dad showed up?" I asked.

"He would have shot him," Mom said, "that's what." She laughed sharply, her cue that she was ready to change the subject. "Oh, you don't even want to know. Your poor grandmother, she put up with a lot. Grampa put her through a lot."

"By her hair, down the steps?" *Gramma? Not Gramma!*

"That was all a long time ago," my mother said. "That's all in the past."

No, it's not. Right across the room was that kitchen table. Our story had been hiding in plain sight for years.

What happened next was that in June, I closed on the house. In mid-August, I got divorced. Two years later, I began my application to adopt my child. Now, from a distance of twenty-four years, when I look back, those three events—house purchase, divorce, adoption—line up as naturally as stars in a constellation.

What I didn't realize at the time was that as I moved forward, I was blatantly committing the betrayal I had always feared a man might commit against me. *I* was the one who shifted my gaze away from my marriage, who found a more compelling vision. *I* was the one who turned toward a new love and went after it with all my heart. I was convinced then, and still am now, that it was necessary to leave my volatile marriage before I had a child.

And due to my particular set of circumstances, single-motherhood was an option for me. I was a financially independent, educated, and employed white woman living at the tail end of the twentieth century. I could divorce, claim single-motherhood-by-choice, and suffer no stigma. I would not be ostracized the way unmarried mothers used to be, the way many marginalized and minority women still are. Aware of my lucky breaks, and humbled by that awareness, I filed divorce papers.

How I dreaded the actual divorce date, but on a Monday morning two weeks before our third wedding anniversary, we showed up at the courthouse for our proceedings, which took less time than a drive-through car wash. Afterward, my husband—my ex-husband—walked me to the parking lot, and we hugged. I was driving a rented van we'd packed full the night before with the last boxes I'd left at his house. I was exhausted.

"I'm following you home," he said. "You're too tired to drive all that way by yourself."

It made no sense, his driving to Omaha after our divorce, but I heard myself say, "Okay. Thanks."

Late that evening, we got to my new house, and he slept downstairs on the daybed in the sunroom. The next day, he helped me unpack the van. Afterward, tired, we lay on my couch together and, as I'd done a million times over the past three years, I dipped my face into his neck. Had we taken off our wedding rings by now?

"I still love you, you know." We both said this.

One day's help turned into a couple days' visit. With the divorce decision out of our way, we were free to talk as easily as when we'd first spent time together, and as openly as I'd wished we could have in marriage. Released from any vows, I was more myself, and I felt a flood of compassion for the man—*poet* again, not *husband*—resting with me on my couch. In that serene moment, I realized how anxious I'd been in marriage. Was it our particular marriage, or would any marriage leave me feeling like a stranger to my strengths? The question saddened me. I might never have another chance.

But unlike my mother and grandmother, if I wanted to, I could try again. When I was young, Gramma Stella had told me, "Divorce is no good, but better divorced than never married." Over the years I'd wondered if she'd meant this as a warning against becoming an old maid; or perhaps in her world, "never married" meant never knowing sexual intimacy and, for all her anguish, she felt that that knowledge was essential to a fully lived life. As I talked calmly with the poet in the aftermath of our divorce, I agreed with Gramma, "Better divorced than never married."

And just as I was settling into our new, wondrous circumstances—deep affection with lots of breathing space—he told me, "There's some news you'll be interested in."

"Yeah?"

It was about Dr. X.—the "red flag" psychiatrist.

"He was arrested." At a pharmacy, as he'd tried to have a prescription filled for himself. I'd known there was something "not right" about him, but there was no satisfaction in hearing this news, just a deep plunge in my gut.

"You know," I said, "he was really destructive to our marriage."

"I knew you'd say that."

"But he was. Destructive." As I said this, I knew there was the possibility the poet might lash out in defense of Dr. X., who, for all his faults, had offered the poet support and acceptance, and that feeling of connection had stayed with him, which was good. But if he did lash out, I could ask him to, please, leave my house. We were now divorced.

There was no rage, just silence. Summer was winding down, the cicadas circling the house were insistent, and it was too late to talk about how things might have been different for us if Dr. X. had been more helpful—or less harmful. There was no point now.

The poet left the next day, but after he got home, we indulged in long emails and phone calls, and tried to ignore the irony that in the aftermath of divorce, we were turning to each other for comfort. Unsure if we were being brave or rash, in October we decided it would be okay if he drove back up to Omaha for a weekend visit.

Is anything lovelier than reconciliation? You both say such gentle things. You treat each other to sweet, small attentions. You offer favors, half your dessert. In fact, on the second night of the poet's visit, I offered my whole dessert. "Really," I said, sliding over my plate of pie, "you're welcome to it."

I felt a fever coming on. Abdominal pains, which rapidly got worse, wrapped across my middle and swung around to my back. The only doctor I knew in town was someone I privately referred to as "the fertility goddess" because I'd consulted with her a few times about fertility treatments, but she was away at a conference. The poet took me to the ER, where they confirmed what I'd suspected: A fibroid tumor discovered during my pregnancies was now infected. I was admitted for major IV antibiotics. The poet canceled his classes and stayed with me until my doctor returned. "That fibroid has to be removed," she told us. "I'll operate next Monday. You can go home until then." Offhand, she added, "But you'll need to continue the antibiotics through the weekend."

"Okay. If you'll call in the prescription, we can pick it up on the way home."

"Oh, no, you need IV meds," she said.

I was confused. "A nurse comes to the house?"

"No nurse," Dr. Fertility Goddess scoffed. "You two can do it."

"No, we can't. We're writers." When I had the chance, I pulled her aside. "We just got divorced. We don't always get along. We're not medical people." For emphasis, I added, "He's a poet."

"Oh, come on." Dr. Goddess actually laughed. "You two, I'm not worried about. You should see some of the people who go home with these procedures. Really, it's easy."

It was complicated. I arrived home with a needle and IV port inserted into the top of my hand and taped to my skin. A nurse came once to show us the ropes, and then she left. For each treatment, the poet had to attach tubing to the port and flush it out by injecting a syringe of saline solution. After he administered the antibiotic, he had to flush out the line again with another injection. There were two drugs, each given within one hour of the other, four times daily. The first at 6 a.m., the last at midnight. For four days, the poet set his alarm for the early-morning treatments. We were both bleary-eyed when he came downstairs to the sunroom where I was set up, but he was unfailingly upbeat. Flushing the line was the scariest part: We meticulously followed the nurse's notes each time. Watching his precision as he filled the syringe and flicked it to dislodge air bubbles, I admired his steady hands, those lovely hands. "I'm sorry you got stuck doing this," I whispered. "You're a good nurse."

"I'm glad I'm here," he whispered back.

As he completed each of the treatments successfully, we were giddy with relief. We laughed a lot that weekend, but we never stopped being frightened. We were in over our heads. We were divorced.

And yet, during those days, I felt profoundly married. How easy it suddenly seemed—to be not only in love but also in alliance, to have each other's back. During marriage, many doors had slammed shut on us, and we had slammed doors on each other. But now, postdivorce, I finally felt admitted into the deep heart of the secret of what goes on between two people when they conceive a new life—conceive as in *visualize, believe in*. Were we finding a new way to be together? If so, how could this potent feeling—at once newborn and sage—not bring forth something as monumental as family? I remember thinking, *If I ever do manage to have children,* this *kind of love is the air I want them to breathe daily.* I wondered if this giddiness was what my parents had felt when they reconciled after their long separation. I hoped so.

Every few weekends, we visited in the poet's town or mine. Friends who had held my hand while I went through divorce were now asking, "What is going on?"

My mother was incredulous. "After everything you've been through, how can you go back to him?"

She was holding me accountable. I didn't know what to say. "It'll be fine, Mom."

In a calmer voice, she asked, "Can you tell me what you're trying to do? What are you trying to accomplish?"

I had no idea, I just knew that our reunion was powerful and beyond logic. Trying to wrap up that phone call, make my mother laugh, I asked, "So, are you going to stop loving me if I end up getting back together with him?"

A beat of silence. "No." Her voice was resigned. "I'd probably love you more."

Months down the road in our fragile reconciliation, the poet and I realized one reason we'd felt compelled to come together postdivorce was that we couldn't move forward in any direction—alone or together—until we mourned our lost babies.

"What we should do," he said one day, "is plant a memorial garden."

And so we did, in my backyard. Rather than daisies or other flowers more commonly associated with infants, I chose irises. Those complicated inside-out blooms seemed more appropriate.

During this time, I also began a practice of simple meditation. For a few minutes before going to bed, sitting cross-legged before a lit candle, eyes closed, I'd inhale and think *baby,* and then exhale and think *baby.* Some breaths were a hello to the child I longed for, some were goodbye to those I'd lost.

*

One morning as I was getting ready for work, I heard on the local NPR station an announcement for an information session at an agency for international adoption. I had, of course, thought about adoption, and though I wished I could embrace that option, it didn't resonate with me the way pregnancy did. The truth was, adoption intimidated me. I didn't believe I had the necessary stamina. And would an agency even work with a single parent?

To confirm for myself that adoption was not a viable choice, I went to the info session. Turns out, the agency did work with single parents, facilitating adoptions in Asia and South America. I wished I were ready to consider adoption, but I knew I wasn't and might never be. And yet, as I sat in my folding chair, these words—these exact words—passed through me: *I'm going to have a son born in Vietnam.*

That's wishful thinking, I told myself.

In that evening's group, I was the only single person. As I looked over the couples, I imagined them living peaceful home lives. What secret bonding agent united them so powerfully that they could step forward and do something as monumental as adopt a child together? Mulling over these questions, scribbling on the handouts, I stayed until the end of the session, thanked the speakers, and left.

Six months later, I got a phone call. "Hey, this is Cheryl from the adoption agency. You attended an info session here last spring on international adoption, and I'm not sure where you are now, but at the time you seemed really interested . . ."

I did?

The agency was having a weekend workshop soon. I listened to the details and, to be polite, wrote down the date, then tucked the scrap of paper into a pile on the kitchen counter.

A Sunday morning not long after, I was on the phone with the poet, staring out the kitchen window onto my messy, overgrown backyard—my house, after I bought it, was never as put-together as I'd envisioned it in my reveries—and I admitted to him that I was making lists of all the opportunities available to me if I lived out my days as a childless person. I could travel, live in Paris, wear cashmere, and he told me that all sounded good.

"But I can't do it." I started crying. "I can't give up the idea of being a mother."

"But you shouldn't give it up," he said. "You already are a mother. You just have to figure out how to make it happen."

After so many failures, he still believed I had a chance. If I was, as he said, *already* a mother, didn't that qualify me to step in and sweep my arms around an *already born* baby who needed a mother? *You are a mother.* It was with those words spoken by my ex-husband that the seed of the idea of adoption was firmly planted.

One stumbling block I had with adoption was the intimacy of it. Blunt truth: I was afraid another woman's child might be too *other*. While holding her baby, would I search for the mother's secrets in the baby's face, or would I long for the details of my family's features? And what if I couldn't cozy up to the scent of a stranger's child? Would I be ready when it was time to lift my baby from the bedding and cloths—possibly dirty, soiled—he or she had been kept in? I was ashamed of my squeamishness, but I had to admit it to myself. How else could I figure out if I was capable?

At the adoption workshop, the opening discussion was about loss. The agency director, Cheryl, told us, "For babies who are adopted, life has not taught them consistency."

Even for babies who, just minutes after birth, land in the arms of eager adoptive parents or attentive foster parents or conscientious caregivers, there is the staggering loss of the birth mother's body and voice. In utero, the baby lived for months hearing that voice, and now it's gone. For babies in orphanages, there may or may not be timely feedings. The baby might be held and spoken to during feedings, or the bottle might be propped.

And in time, whether the orphaned baby receives excellent care or negligent care, there will be one more unpredictable rupture when the baby is taken from the now-familiar atmosphere of the orphanage and put into the arms of the adoptive parents. If those parents are from a different culture, the baby may no longer hear their native language—one more loss. The new parents' voices make strange sounds; their scents are an onslaught of the unknown. The adopted baby experiences incalculable losses and changes, each one as unpredictable as an earthquake. *Sideswiped*.

"Think of the five most important things in your life," Cheryl prompted us. I listed my health, creativity, family, friends, and home.

"Now, cross out one of them," Cheryl said. "What would it be like to lose that?" There were about a dozen of us in the room. We sat quietly, not looking up. "Now cross out another of your five important things." And she continued until we had crossed off everything we cherished. "That's how the world feels to an adopted baby. That baby has lost everything."

By now, within me, the paradigm shift had happened. All I could think about was how strange and terrifying the sound and size and scent of the adoptive parent must be *for the baby*. What would I do to soothe that baby? *Anything in my power*. At the end of the weekend workshop, I began the next stage in the journey toward my child, who would be born in Vietnam.

Chapter 17

Our Red Suitcase

> *It is entirely possible*
> *That we are islands in the territory of angels.*
> —"Innocentii," Mary O'Malley

By now it was mid-2000, four and a half years after my first miscarriage, almost two years since divorce, and a little less than two years since the poet and I had reconciled. He was still the person I reviewed my day with by telephone most nights, but now we visited less often. I was busy assembling my adoption application.

In June, the adoption agency sent my completed application to Vietnam, and, at work, I submitted my request for parental leave. I knew I would need to give the baby consistent, wraparound care, right from the start. To foster attachment, I got a Guatemalan baby sling so I could keep the baby close to my body. I took a Red Cross first-aid class and replaced the kitchen fire extinguisher. A friend had loaned me a high chair, which was already set up in my kitchen. I was shopping for the safest car seat.

Did the distance between the poet and me set in when he visited and saw all the baby equipment? Did he feel left out? Bored? And was I kidding myself? I had ended our marriage and opted for single-motherhood, yet I hoped that he, in some murky role as "friend of the family," would stay by my side. Was there logic in that?

Still, in the contrary way couples sometimes operate, rather than discuss the growing distance between us, we decided to take a trip to the small Maine town where his family had vacationed when he was a kid. We flew into Manchester, New Hampshire, and on our drive into Maine, I insisted on pulling off at the Kittery Outlets to look for discounted onesies at Carter's Babies & Kids. Those tiny cotton garments made my fingers so happy.

As we continued our drive north, I was annoyed by how fast the poet was driving. My complaints angered him. When we arrived at our inn, we were still speaking to each other, but not so nicely. The next morning, across the narrow road and down a slight slope, I found a dock and sat there alone for hours. To be as close to the water as possible, as if cozying up to a friend, I sat on the planks and pulled my journal from the pocket of my denim jacket. It was cool enough for a jacket in July. For several pages, I vented my frustration with the poet and my disappointment in myself. But when I looked up, I saw that the landscape was a triptych all around me. The poet had brought me to an exceptionally pretty place.

To my left, at the harbor's mouth, sailboats inched by against a blue sky. Directly across the harbor, on a green slope, a small white house and a larger red one were etched against the grass. To my right, at the base of the harbor, lobster boats bobbed while lobstermen prepared to go out into their day. Ropes tossed from docks plunked into the bellies of rowboats. Chains clanked. Dinghies marked the spots from which the early-morning lobster boats had departed. Brightly striped buoys tilted, floated. The light was crystalline, the scent was seaweed, the sea air unmuffled by humidity.

I didn't know it at the time, but I was falling in love again. In years to come, I would return to this harbor often. This landscape would imprint itself on me so deeply that back in Omaha, in winter, I would need only to pick up a beach stone from the small pile on my desk and hold it in my palm to feel the serenity that came to me that first day when I sat on the dock alone. In Maine, water met land in a way that was different from the Calabrian coast. Cool and austere, the Maine coast wasn't sexy or provocative. The view I took in was a private aesthetic, personal to me. I had arrived here without my family. My breathing was calm, moored. I listened to the water gulping against the posts below the dock. Four seagulls assembled on the harbor's surface; a fifth dove under, and the others screeched. I felt sun on my face.

Over the next days, as we drove around the peninsula, I wrote down addresses and phone numbers from FOR RENT signs. I didn't know what would happen to the poet and me as a couple, but I knew I was coming back to this harbor. I wanted this place to figure into the perfect future of my baby-to-be.

That small town in Maine was the poet's last gift to me, and I treasure it. On our return from that vacation, we had one last fiery scene in my house. *It's easier to leave angry.*

As the poet exited our argument, I listened to his footsteps on the planks of my front porch. I could have stopped him but knew I shouldn't, and so I didn't. As a mother-to-be, I had less tolerance for my ambivalence. From that day, we moved on separately to the next lives we were meant to live. A few years later, I heard he had remarried. I wish him only well, as I do his sons, who are now men and thriving.

For parental leave, my university granted "a period of eight weeks paid disability leave (pre-and postpartum) for absences associated with pregnancy and childbirth," so I submitted a request for eight weeks, which my department and dean approved. But a few weeks later, someone in an admin office called me to say that as an adoptive mother, I did not qualify for parental leave, which was considered disability leave. There was no disability associated with adoption. For adoptive parents, a two-week leave was granted "to provide care and assistance to the child."

Two weeks? The round trip to Vietnam and back would take that long or more. And what about time for the all-important attachment process? "This policy is saying that my adopted child is less deserving than a birth child," I told my dean.

By now, I was 44 and tired. For over two decades, I'd been carving a life far from what my traditional Italian family had expected. I'd left home to work in New York and live on my own, and I'd done it not to be eccentric but to follow my heart. I'd left the nine-to-five work world to write a novel. I'd loved men I didn't marry when marriage didn't seem right. When I finally did marry, I divorced because I was determined to create the steadiest home possible for my child. *I want to raise a child.* I might have seemed radical in my family's eyes, but at heart I was a traditionalist. I was not taking motherhood or adoption lightly. My adoption agency had educated me: I knew what my child needed. I was crying when I said to my dean—I trusted her enough to cry in front of her—"Adoption is not a second-class family experience."

"Your child is *not* less deserving. You do need to get that leave."

I had good people in my corner, but this was my fight to fight. I put aside the manuscript I was working on, and my parental leave campaign became my summer's work. I met with or sent letters to state senators, members of the university's Board of Regents, university lawyers and private lawyers, my on-campus union rep, psychologists, social workers, medical doctors, news reporters, and colleagues across campus who had recently become parents. Meanwhile, the adoption process inched forward. Days, months, waiting.

At least I wasn't waiting alone—my mother was now my neighbor in Omaha for part of the year. Though she'd tried valiantly, living alone in Florida, far from family, was not working for her. "Summer's the worst! No one's around," she lamented. My dad was six years gone, and she was still annoyed with him. "I told your father I didn't want to live in Florida full-time, but he had to move down here lock, stock, and barrel."

After those phone calls, I'd wake in the middle of the night and feel in my bones that my 70-year-old mother on her own in Florida was, for us, just not right. I asked her to consider coming to Omaha for the summer months. She moved into a little apartment in a 1960s high-rise four blocks from my house, and she made friends in her building quickly, going to the theater with one group, crocheting with another, and Saturday was movie night. We had dinner together a few nights a week. Together, Mom and I were unabashedly eager for the arrival of my baby. If it were sixty years earlier and we lived in Vazzano, we'd have been weaving and needlepointing as Gramma Stella had while waiting for that letter from Grampa.

*

At work, I finally got the good news that the Regents had "expanded the university adoption leave policy for faculty and staff," granting the primary caregiver for an adopted child up to eight weeks of leave, equal to the time granted to birth parents. This new policy applied to both female and male employees. The bylaws had been changed for the entire system, which included four campuses. "Well," a friend told me, "that explains why you needed to move to Nebraska. You had to get that done." Several of the administrators I'd talked with during my campaign contacted me to say they were pleased with the results, and they gave me their best wishes.

Now the baby just needed to get here.

And then one sunny October dawn, I was standing at the kitchen sink preparing the teapot, and a gleam of light bounced off the corner of my neighbors' roof—sunbeam meeting gutter—and within that moment I felt the compact weight of a child in my arms, could almost see tiny fingers pointing, so I explained, *That's our neighbors' house, it's morning, that's sunlight.* My baby was moving toward me.

On Halloween, I had an appointment at the adoption agency to review paperwork. Rainy morning. When I rushed into the office with a dripping umbrella, my adoption counselor, Kristi, held up a laminated email: my official referral. My baby was born. He was almost 1 month old. Healthy.

"When do I go get him? When?"

"Soon, we hope," Kristi said. "There's no way of knowing at this point."

All day I made phone calls to the archipelago of my spread-out family and friends, announcing *Leo! Baby Leo!* On the official adoption papers, he would have three middle names: Alfredo, like my father; and the two Vietnamese names he was given at the orphanage. I chose his first name, Leo, as a nod to Tolstoy, whose novels I admired for their wide worldview. That's what I wished for my son—a panoramic perspective. I hoped he'd be made strong by the blending of his

Vietnamese heritage and our Italian ancestry as he grew up with a single mother on the Midwestern Plains.

The orphanage sent us a few photos of Leo. *So beautiful!* I studied the background for details of his life in Vietnam. Finally, on a Tuesday in late January, I was walking out of my office to teach my one o'clock class and my phone rang. It was Cheryl: "You're cleared to travel."

"When do I go?" *Now? Today?*

"As soon as you possibly can. Here's the number for the travel agent. Call her!"

I ran downstairs to my class and couldn't contain myself. "Wait till I tell you guys what just happened!"

From Gramma Stella, I had learned to honor good-luck gestures, so for my trip to Hanoi to adopt Leo, I chose a red suitcase because red is a good-luck color in Vietnam. Baby clothes, diapers, and bottles were stacked on Gramma's green dining table, and as I packed, I whispered over and over, like an incantation, "Leo, Leo, Leo."

He was 4 months old the day he was put in my arms, wearing a powder-blue pom-pom cap tugged down to his eyebrows. Below the rim of the hat, his tiny face was not pleased. At the orphanage, he wouldn't look at me—but that was good. His withdrawal from me, a stranger, meant he was attached to his current caregivers. This was cause for relief. If, after the trauma of separation from his birth mother, he could attach once, chances were good he'd be able to attach again.

Our first night in the hotel, Leo cried. And cried. For long hours he was inconsolable, and I ached for him. Within his twelve-pound body, so much disruption had been absorbed. He wept and I held him, murmuring reassurance, whispering poems, anything I could think of, in the lowest voice possible so he wouldn't be frightened but to assure him that he wasn't alone. As we walked up and down our narrow, red-carpeted hotel room, I eventually discovered that the bathroom's overhead light caught his eye, so we stood in the tiny bathroom for a long time, then we left. And returned. When I turned on the faucet, the running water grabbed his attention, so we listened to the water, and when I dipped his fingers into it, he was fascinated enough to stop crying for a while. These moments were my introduction to one of Leo's most distinctive characteristics: his curiosity. How heartened I was to see that, within himself, he had the power to interrupt his own heartache. During my long wait for adoption, I'd made all kinds of pledges to the universe. *I will do everything, anything, all things possible to keep my baby safe.* Heartfelt vows, but abstract. Now, as I held my son, the actual, highly individualized human being—his puffy cheeks, alertness, and stern gaze—the enormity of the stakes took my breath away.

And yet I wasn't afraid. Never in the face of love had I felt so sure of myself. My mother-love would inoculate him. I *was* going to do whatever it took to keep him safe and healthy, I promised him. Silently, I also promised his birth parents, two people neither Leo nor I would likely ever have the chance to meet. And I warned myself: *You do whatever you need to do to take care of your own hurt heart and keep your leftover sadness away from him.*

After many hours of pacing, I opened our tall balcony door, pushed out the shutters, and the sun was rising onto our first full day as a family. Leo stopped crying, and when I looked down at him in my arms, he smiled at me. Just a speck of a smile but definitely a smile. "See?" I whispered. "We're going to be okay."

Overall, we've been much more than okay. Leo is college-age now, and our home life has been sweet. Our Omaha neighborhood is as lively as a small village, and during summers and holidays, we've traveled to be with our family and far-off friends. Not every summer but as often as possible we go to Maine, to a cabin on that harbor my ex-husband brought me to years ago. Our compact family of two is not only the greatest gift of my life, it also feels plain normal.

But the week of his sixth birthday, Leo did crawl onto my lap one evening to tell me how much he wished he had a father. I held him and said, "You're right. It's sad that our family doesn't have a dad. I feel that, too." Then I told him that in every family—indeed, in every life—there is at least one sadness, some deep difficulty, and the absence of a father was a sadness in our family life. I reminded him there were several wonderful men—his uncle, our cousins, and family friends—who brought us a lot of happiness; plus, we had each other.

"I know, but I'm going to have a dad," he insisted. And just as I was taking a breath to figure out what to say next, Leo added, "I just hope he parks in the right place," and I laughed. He was referring to our narrow driveway, where our Honda sits comfortably but if guests don't park just so, we can't back out. What I heard him saying was that as much as he longed for a father, he didn't want anyone to mess up what we already have, because he was happy with that.

My choice to be a single parent was premised on a big gamble: By raising my son outside of marriage, I could protect him from witnessing certain strains of heartache, and then maybe, when he was grown, he'd be better able to make a happy union with a life partner, which was one thing I simply could not model for him.

Meanwhile, I did what came naturally. I swathed my son with love.

And, wisely, as he got older, he reminded me in different ways that his life was his and that he needed to go into the world on his terms, not mine. One day I was driving him to day camp and glanced in the rearview mirror as he read the cartoons and notes I'd scribbled onto his lunch sack. Gently, he advised me, "Tomorrow it might be better if you don't write so much on my bag."

"How come?" I asked.

"People might get the impression you care about me too much."

Again, he'd made me laugh. But later, throughout that day, I felt a twinge of accusation—unjust accusation, mild shame, as if I'd been called out, but on something I could do very little about. Was this how Nonno Paolo had felt when the women of Vazzano suspected that his overzealous love for Alfredo had soured into the evil eye? As a mother, I was starting to feel compassion for the overvigilant adults who'd raised me. Gramma and Grampa had gone to great lengths to arrange a transatlantic marriage for Catherine, to ensure she'd be cared for after they were gone.

But there were other ways to care for our kids. What if my grandparents had stepped back, granted Catherine agency, supported her as she learned to manage her own health care, allowed her to find her own spouse?

For Leo's benefit, it was time for me to separate from our family's template. Our native anxiety had been forged in extremis: during wartime, earthquakes, transatlantic migration. Panic may have been appropriate then, but it was now a vestigial reflex, more damaging than helpful. Psychologist Erik Erikson, in his writings on the stages of psychosocial development, talks about establishing a correct *ratio* of trust and distrust in our societal interactions. "When we enter a situation, we must be able to differentiate how much we can trust and how much we must mistrust . . . This, too, is certainly a part of the animal's instinctive equipment." I had the distrust covered; but now my son—my healthy son—was prompting me to allow breathing room for trust. Perhaps Leo was reiterating Howard's long-ago message, telling me, *It's time to separate.*

Chapter 18

Nonna Catherine

> *'Na mamma fa pe centu figji, ma centu figji no fannu pe 'na mamma.*
>
> *One mother can take care of a hundred children, but a hundred children can't take care of one mother.*
> —a saying from Vazzano

During the ten years my mother had an apartment in Omaha, she lived a more-or-less daily family life with Leo and me. Her love for him was grander than anything I could have wished for him, and now, for the rest of his life, he has Nonna Catherine in his heart.

In essence, my mother became my partner in raising Leo. When he was a baby, I was still working toward tenure and writing my second novel, and my mother held Leo for hours. When I became department chair, with lots of deadlines, Leo was a toddler obsessed with trains, so my mother learned the names of all of Thomas the Tank Engine's friends in the roundhouse. In time, I sold my second novel and had months of revisions; by then, Leo had taught Nonna the names of his Transformers. He was proud that she could distinguish the Autobots from the Decepticons. I'd never seen her happier.

And she was good to me, too—calling to wish me well on the first day of each semester, never letting me pay when we ate out together. When we drove anywhere, I was the chauffeur up front while Mom and Leo sat in the back, holding hands. She was always available to babysit, and there was no one on the planet I trusted more to care for my son.

We were a family of three, and our circle felt complete.

She was not pleased when, the summer before Leo entered second grade, he and I got a dog. "You need that dog like you need a hole in your head," my mother told me when we brought PJ home. Our breed of Southern Italian peasants does not have a weakness for the house pet stamped onto its DNA. In Vazzano, the family's donkey was used for transportation and farmwork. Nonna Anna kept hens in a coop across the road from her house. She'd slit the neck of a fowl, and a few hours later, we'd all sit down to a platter of roasted chicken. No one winced; we dug in. In short, I grew up believing that if animals were not useful or tasty, they should be categorized with mosquitoes and ticks.

But Leo was the kind of kid who ran up to any passing canine and extended his palm to be sniffed, ready to make friends. Occasionally I gave in, and we would visit the Humane Society, and on one of those occasions, PJ, a white- and brown-spotted shih tzu mix, origins unknown, chose us.

"You're not letting that dog into the bedrooms, are you?" Mom asked.

But it didn't take long. For PJ's first Christmas with us, Nonna Catherine gave him a tiny red turtleneck sweater. When Mom sat in her favorite chair, PJ curled up at her feet as she leaned down to pet him. Quickly she went from barely tolerating our dog to accepting him because Leo loved him, and then to loving PJ just because she did.

My mother opened up in remarkable ways during her years in Omaha. After decades of keeping a strategic distance from her, I was surprised by how natural it felt—and how comforting—to tell my friends, "We're having dinner with my mother tonight." It made me inordinately happy to overhear her now and then tell Leo, "Look what a good lunch your mommy made for you." Golden times. We had a lot of them.

So it still bewilders me that there were also times when Leo asked, "Why do you and Nonna bicker?"

Me, through clenched teeth: "We're *not* bickering. I'm just trying to explain to your grandmother I *will* call about her doctor's appointment [or phone bill, eyeglasses, prescription] as soon as I have a free minute."

My mother, head tilted, martyr-like: "All I'm asking is for a phone call."

Me: "Do you realize I have a child, a job, a house—"

Her: "Oh, give me a break."

Me: "No, you give *me* a break."

During her last years, I tried to find doctors who could alleviate her ailments. I tried to organize her paperwork, facilitate her social life, prepare foods she enjoyed. I claim no altruism in this. As a daughter, I was and always had been as self-involved as any other child—which meant that every time I saw on her face or heard in her voice that, despite my earnest efforts, despite the fact that she had *me* at the center of her universe, she still wasn't happy, I believed I had failed. From *I've failed*, it was a short drop to *I'm a failure*. This pattern of effort–frustration–failure was the endless loop of how it felt to love my mother. This was how we were tethered. That never changed.

In 2008, my mother turned 78. She needed a walker because she'd had several falls, but she was still front row for Leo's piano recitals and tae kwon do tests. More than a year passed, and then I realized she wasn't heating up the meals I put in her freezer. She didn't have the energy. When I suggested assisted living, she told me, "No way. Don't you dare."

"Can you two stop bickering?" Leo asked.

And then the night before Easter, Mom walked a few steps into the hallway outside her apartment to leave a gift card for the kid who delivered her Sunday newspaper—an unnecessary and kind gesture—but she ventured out without her walker and fell. She was in the hospital for a week, followed by almost a month in a medical-rehab center.

A few days before her scheduled release, we had a meeting set with her rehab team, but when I arrived, she was on oxygen. "Something bronchial is going on," the nurse said. "We can't discharge her till this is cleared up."

My mother protested and wanted to go home. *But how can I take care of you at home?* As if she could read my thoughts, she said, "I am *not* going to assisted living, do you hear me?"

"We'll see, Mom, we'll see." That evening, I'd brought Leo and PJ with me, and they were visiting patients' rooms while I sat cross-legged in the chair by Mom's bed, grading my students' final papers.

Instinctively, I knew we were at a new threshold; it was time to direct all my energy toward my mother.

That night, as frequently happened, I had dreams in which my mother and I were furious with each other.

The next morning, Thursday, as I waited for the doctor's call, I found myself unable to leave my kitchen. The fridge was full of ingredients that had accumulated when the last weeks of my semester coincided with Mom's month in rehab. I chopped the plume off an almost-too-ripe pineapple, dug out Gramma Stella's cast-iron skillet, and mixed the ingredients for a pineapple upside-down cake from *Joy of Cooking*. My page was marked with a gift receipt dated 1981, the year Mom had given me the book for Christmas. While the oven was hot, I roasted golden beets. I cleaned the artichokes that had been on sale at Whole Foods ten days earlier. I considered stuffing the artichokes—one of my mother's specialties—but that takes time, and I couldn't shake the feeling that I was working against the clock.

This weekend would be Mother's Day. My brother and my oldest niece were flying in for a visit. They would be here for only a few meals, but I kept cooking as compulsively (though not as expertly) as my mother used to before Paul and I came home from college.

I chopped up two bruised apples and a ripened pear and let them simmer with honey and lemon juice, a variation of the applesauce Mom used to make. I was on a mission to showcase whatever freshness could be eked out of those foods that were turning bad. Peeling, stirring, tasting, I listened to an NPR *Fresh Air* podcast of Terry Gross interviewing Burt Bacharach and Hal David, who co-wrote many of the sixties hits that were the soundtrack of my youth. When they played a snippet of Dionne Warwick singing "Promises, Promises," I started to cry. Aretha Franklin sang "Say a Little Prayer," and I was weeping.

If my mother, propped up in her recliner in Room 107, were hearing these songs, she would have been unmoved. What had emotional significance for one of us rarely resonated for the other. So it was with surprise and some chagrin that I found myself crying ("Someday you'll cry," she used to yell at me, "and it'll be too late!").

Aretha's "Say a Little Prayer" was bringing me back to my parents' parties on the patio. Suddenly I saw Catherine dressed up and smiling—really smiling. God, she gave good parties. People told her that all the time. Did she hear it? Believe it?

I considered driving out to have lunch with my mother, but the sad truth was that cooking alone in my kitchen, I felt closer to her than I would have sitting by her bed, where we'd likely squabble. The shocking truth was that I wanted to be close to her. Bottom-line truth: It was too late. It had almost always been too late.

When the *Fresh Air* interview was over, I found a YouTube video of Dionne Warwick singing "Walk on By." Her outfit was something Mom would have worn to a dinner dance in the sixties: straight ankle-length black skirt and a sequined sleeveless top; a cool, classy look that my mother pulled off and that *almost* passed her off as the composed and competent woman I once believed she was—a woman she could have been if she herself had believed it possible. I would never understand: After the misfortunes of her youth, she was brave enough to undergo three open-heart surgeries, initiate the reconciliation with my father, give birth twice. During the years of my dad's illnesses, she cared for him meticulously despite her anger. Why couldn't she live more fully in the life—and the love—she'd earned for herself?

Singing in the YouTube window, Dionne wandered among a dozen or so "mod" black swivel chairs arranged (somewhat absurdly) here and there on a white set. The slit of her tight skirt was so slight, her strides were tiny and constricted. Absently spinning a chair, she picked a path across the stage in her pointy high heels. It was so early sixties, the combination of high glamour and practiced nonchalance. Toward the end of "Walk on By," Dionne's fingers rose to her brow in a small salute, an awkward gesture made even more awkward by the jolting quality of the download. It was in this pantomimed farewell that I understood two things clearly. First, I'd been kidding myself. My mother's passing from this world was going to sadden me more than I'd allowed myself to even begin to imagine. Second, sad as her death would be, she and I had said our most wrenching goodbye a long time ago.

*

She died just before dawn on the Monday after Mother's Day. On Saturday night, she'd been taken from the rehab center to the hospital, where my brother, my niece, Leo, and I stayed with her round the clock. At one point during her last hours, I found myself alone at her bedside. "Mom," I whispered, "if you forgive me, I forgive you." I had to believe she was able to hear me. "I love you. I'm so sorry it was the way it was for us. Thank you for everything. You worked really hard."

Two days later, as I hurriedly got ready for our flight to Pittsburgh for the funeral—she'd be buried with my dad and next to my grandparents—PJ did something he'd never done. In our backyard, he rolled in the mud and his morning poop, covered himself in it, a show of grief so raw I couldn't be angry, just very sad for all of us.

During the flight to Pittsburgh, I thought of the labyrinthine obstacles Catherine's heart had encountered. All her life she'd been lucky enough to know that her family and friends loved her, but what eluded her was the feeling of being loved. I believe that changed in her later years as she helped me raise Leo. I hope it did. Allowing herself to actually feel loved had been my mother's life's work.

Chapter 19

The Basement

> *Do not be daunted by the enormity of the world's grief. Do justly NOW. Love mercy NOW. Walk humbly NOW. You are not obligated to complete the work but neither are you free to abandon it.*
> —*The Talmud*

After my mother died, when Leo was unable to sleep after I tucked him in, he'd come downstairs and find me reading, and I could tell by the look on his face—"You miss Nonna"—and we'd cry together. On his bed, he had three quilts she'd crocheted for him. "Can PJ sleep in my bed with me?" he asked.

"Yes," I said, "of course."

For me, as when my father died, the shock of losing my mother sunk in deeper with time, pain saturating me as I realized her absence was permanent. There was no getting around the fact that my days were easier and I slept more soundly now that I wasn't always on alert for an emergency phone call, but I missed her.

In the fall, a friend urged me to use my newfound free time to go on Match.com, and, to my surprise, I started dating someone for the first time in years. The man was in Omaha only part-time, which was perfect: My life was too busy for a full-time boyfriend. Things started out promising, but by New Year's, we were tangled up in volleys of disagreement: "What did you say?" "No, what did *you* say, and what did you mean?" Mutually, we decided to give it a bit of a break.

He had to go out of town in early January, a planned departure, but to my shock, I plummeted and felt eviscerated by loss. Worse than loss—I felt culpable for what I'd lost. *I made it all go bad.* This level of upset far exceeded the circumstances. Nice guy, but I'd known him only six months. Now that my son was the axis for my life, I couldn't believe a failing relationship had the power to derail me, but I was derailed. Short of breath. Rapid heart rate. Unable to sleep. I was slipping down again into my "basement."

Basement was the code name my Omaha therapist, Dr. L., and I used for the panic that gripped me when I felt on the brink of losing something—someone—essential to me. *It's my fault. I have to fix this.*

At least by now I had a store of resources to help me—yoga, meditation, walks with my dog, SOS phone calls to friends. When all else failed, I scheduled an extra appointment with Dr. L. When I sat on the couch across from her, she understood immediately. "You've felt this before," she prompted.

"In my marriage sometimes," I said, "and in other relationships."

"And with this recent relationship, you decided to step back and reevaluate, which made sense," Dr. L. said, "but now this old feeling of being abandoned—"

"Yes, yes, I feel abandoned—I know all this, I know." I'd made time to drive myself to her office, but now I couldn't settle into the work. In the window hung a prism that swung in the heat vent's exhaust, sending a rectangle of light onto the wall, then onto the rug. I watched. Dr. L. had been the first therapist to spell it out: *You took on the job of trying to save your mother, but that's an impossible task for a child.*

Spot of light on the wall, the rug. Wall, rug.

"Describe the basement," she said. "What is it like down there this time?"

Usually *basement* summoned up forgotten boxes in my dusty cellar, but today, *basement* was in Braddock, that dirt-floor room below Grampa's bar where he broke the empty liquor bottles. "The ceiling down there was low," I told Dr. L., "like in a cave. He had to smash the bottles. It was part of his work, and then he'd sweep up the broken glass. He was always tidy. But when I picture him doing it, that rough action, I feel bad for how nonverbal he was. When my parents' marriage went so wrong, he must have felt so . . . *stuck.*"

"What comes to my mind now," she said, "when you mention those broken bottles, is a dream you had a few weeks ago."

"Which one?"

"The one with the surgeon? With the glass?"

In that dream, I was watching a surgeon perform a delicate operation. The work was tedious. I couldn't see who the patient was, or even which body part was involved, but the doctor had to use a tiny instrument to extract infinitesimally small slivers of glass.

My breathing slowed as I realized my recent panic was *not* about the current boyfriend. Once again, romance had been the vehicle that delivered me to my psychological *basement*, where I had so many stinging shards to extract, all those bits left over from Braddock.

"There's more work for you to do down there," Dr. L. said. Kindly, she added, "You're doing it already. Even though it's not easy, you're doing it."

Chapter 20

The Diary

> *I hope that things change and that girls will realize that we have millenniums of subservience behind us, that the struggle should continue and that if we lower our guard, it won't take much to eliminate what, at least on paper, four generations of women have with great difficulty gained.*
> —Elena Ferrante, in an interview

The following summer, June 2011, Leo and I traveled to Italy. It was my first time back since both my parents had died. One afternoon as we cleared the table after the midday meal, I dared to bring up my parents' dowry with one of my aunts, and now, probably because my parents and her husband were gone, she whispered to me the details: *"Due milione di lire, da quel tempo."* Two million lire in 1949, the equivalent of $3,200 then; in 2011, equivalent to $30,243. Instead of her usual proper Italian, my aunt slipped into the Calabrian dialect we tend to use when exchanging confidences, and she told me more: *"E 'na casa e u terrenu."* Plus, a house in Vazzano and some land on the outskirts.

As my aunt, sotto voce, disclosed the inventory of the marriage agreement, my cousin, her daughter, was with us, and she asked, "Mamma, are you sure? That's a lot of money." My aunt is dear to me, she's a loving and honest person, but her storytelling does sometimes get as elaborately constructed as her *pasta al forno*. Also, many years had passed, and the story had likely been molded and remolded in many tellings, so I wasn't sure how precise the version Zia had heard was. Basically, though, she corroborated what my mother had said years earlier: Gramma Stella and Grampa Joe offered Alfredo's family a significant dowry. And it was accepted. And, eventually, a quarrel ensued.

My aunt had never heard the story of the car; rather, she'd heard that the feud between father-in-law and son-in-law concerned property papers to a small plot of land that had originally been Gramma's dowry and that Gramma and Grampa had offered as part of Catherine's dowry. My aunt assured me that early on, there was no disagreement between the newlyweds. They were happy. The problem arose between the two men.

Approfittarsene is a powerful notion in our part of Italy. It means "to take advantage of." It's shameful to be seen as someone who takes advantage of others. But even worse is the loss of pride you suffer when someone has taken advantage of you. Made a fool of you. When *approfittarsene* is used, it's with a cynical shaking of the head, which is how both my aunt in Italy and a cousin in Pittsburgh described the next part of the story.

During the six months when Catherine and her parents were in Italy for her betrothal, her father left the bar in the care of two young men in the family circle. In exchange for managing the business, they were invited to live rent-free in the apartment upstairs. Grampa Joe had never forgotten how hard it had been for him and his brother during their first years in Braddock, and he enjoyed helping out the young *paesani*. Maybe Joe's fondness kept him from being as judicious as he should have been.

But six months was a long time, and the guys were inexperienced. Who knows exactly what happened, but when Joe returned from Italy, he found the shelves of his beer garden practically empty and the profits he'd anticipated stripped. *Se ne approfittarono.* Those kids took advantage. According to what I heard, much of the dowry Joe had promised was gone. There was shame in being caught short, and more shame in having been taken advantage of. Was Catherine's father too proud to tell his new son-in-law what had happened? Did he make excuses, leading Alfredo to think the old man was holding out on their agreement? Or did Joe admit what had happened but

Alfredo held him to a hard bargain, and if that was the case, why *wouldn't* Joe get defensive?

I knew where I could probably find answers, but I wasn't ready to look there. Over the years, my mother had threatened me with her diary: "I'm leaving it for you!" When she was still alive and I was preparing her Florida condo for rental, I had found the diary inside a small safe in my parents' bedroom closet. She'd stored it in a plastic ziplock bag with a Post-it note written in her loopy, forced-out-of-left-hand handwriting: *Try seeing Dad for what he was with me . . .* Etc. Right there, I was annoyed. Would she never stop diverting me into these back-alley confrontations, family against family? The sides were never clear, the stakes always high, and there was no possible victory for anyone, just the curdling of our domestic peace, with me soaked in guilt for defending my father and abandoning my mother to her rage.

While she was still alive, I had peeked in the diary and quickly closed it. The first pages charted the early months of my parents' courtship, and young Catherine's enthrallment with the man who would become my father made me cringe. Alfredo was "darling," and her entries perfectly chronicled the self-negating way a girl is capable of abandoning herself in romance. I couldn't be angry with her for having been such a sap—I, too, had been that sap more than once. Rather, I was angry that she'd foisted the diary—and her story—on me.

I cared enough to keep the diary safe in my metal file cabinet but not enough to read it. Then, in December 2011, a few months after Leo and I had returned from Italy, when my mother had been gone one year and seven months, our kitchen floor needed repair. The workmen slid the refrigerator into the dining area, and Gramma's kitchen chairs and a bookcase landed in my office, leaving me only a tiny patch of desk space. PJ's bed was literally under my feet. The dog and I would be confined for four workdays, so I set myself the goal of reading my mother's diary straight through, like a book.

And, as with any powerful book, the diary changed my life.

The lock was tarnished. The brown leather cover was brittle, with FIVE YEAR DIARY embossed in gold lettering. A young girl's keepsake.

The diary was no bigger than my hand. Because each page covered five years, only four lines were allotted to each year. With so little space for her entries, Catherine's handwriting was tiny. I had to use a magnifying glass. I found dried flowers and silly cartoons tucked in here and there. At February 21, 1950, was a postcard of Pittsburgh's William Penn Hotel, where my parents spent their wedding night. Catherine wrote on the postcard "The Very Special & Most Happiest Day of all Days," even though just four days earlier she'd written in her diary, "I tried to speak to him but he gets more angry each time . . . I wonder if you truly love me." Two years later, on the back of that William Penn postcard, she added, "2-22-52. What a silly girl in love I was. I thought I'd have nothing but happiness."

I forced myself back to the very first entry: "Friday, Dec. 24, 1948. At 10:00, a few hours after we arrived at Vazzano Alfredo came and we met. I loved him from the moment that our eyes meet [sic]."

Those simperings continued through their courtship and their "pretend wedding" in Italy. In summer, when she was back in Braddock, she wrote entries every night before bed. Finally, on November 27, at 9:10 p.m., Alfredo arrived at her home. Friends visited until three in the morning. The following days were sweet; the couple listened to records Alfredo had brought from Italy.

But before long, he was often incommunicative. In Vazzano, he'd been so attentive. My guess is that shortly after arriving, Alfredo learned that his father-in-law's resources were less than he'd expected, and that's when the dispute began between the two men. In these early days, though, either Catherine wasn't aware of their discord or she knew and couldn't believe it would affect Alfredo's love for her.

But it did. Though his problem was with her father, Alfredo gave Catherine the silent treatment. Perhaps this was due to their language differences, or the cultural imperative that required a man to stay stern with his wife when he was facing a problem that could not easily be resolved. In late March, the day he left for his job in Yonkers, she felt abandoned: "He left 9 p.m. & kissed me as the rest, not as a wife."

*

Sometimes in his letters from Yonkers, Alfredo was cool, or days passed with no letters at all. Other times, his voice during their rare phone calls was as affectionate as during their courtship, and there had been much affection between them—that was the other news I learned from reading my mother's diary.

By early May, Catherine needed clarification, so she, Gramma Stella, Uncle Jim, and a *compare* with a car left Braddock at two o'clock in the morning and arrived in Yonkers at noon. The men talked to Alfredo—as was customary in these Old World interventions—but Alfredo made no effort to speak with Catherine alone. Who would have blamed her if she'd ended the marriage right then? But she went home, continued writing to him, let time smooth things out. In that way, much like the cycles in my own marriage, my parents' on–off pattern was established.

In July 1950, five months after Alfredo had left, Catherine and her mother were preparing for their annual two weeks in Atlantic City—the doctors recommended the sea air for her health—and Catherine sent Alfredo a letter, as Stella had instructed her, to ask for his permission to travel to Atlantic City with her mother. "He's your husband," her mother told her. "You *have* to ask him!"

Reading this entry, I was furious. The marriage was intended to bring the groom into the New World, with all its freedoms, but now Alfredo was not only Catherine's estranged spouse and lover but also the man who authorized her comings and goings.

In Atlantic City, without Alfredo, Catherine's days were a sandy version of the monotony she lived at home. *Waiting for letters, walks on the boardwalk, more waiting.* But then, out of the blue, Alfredo called to say he had gotten time off and would soon be in Atlantic City. "Honeymoon 2," she wrote in her diary, and I was spooked to read that my parents' early marriage, like mine, was structured around a series of "honeymoons."

In September, Catherine returned to Yonkers and actually interviewed for jobs. No luck, but this visit was "Honeymoon 3."

In October, Alfredo surprised Catherine again, arriving in Braddock the day before her birthday. One morning during "Honeymoon 4," while they lolled late in bed, listening to the radio, Catherine heard her own name announced—her mother had called the radio station and requested a song for Catherine's birthday. How completely surrounded by love she must have felt in that moment. To imagine my parents this happy together was like meeting two new people. How would it have been to grow up with *them*?

For eight days around New Year's: "Honeymoon 5" in Yonkers. While Alfredo worked at the hospital, Catherine rested in his dorm room, and when he had a minute, he'd stop by for a hug. This was news to me. In the puritanical mode of children everywhere, I'd assumed there had been little heat between my parents, especially since their marriage had been arranged, but I was wrong. The fact is, my parents were lovers. Not literally until after their church wedding, of course, but from the start, they were attracted to each other. And even in the adolescent way my mother records the dazzlement of her first love, it's clear the attraction was not one-sided. To learn there had been romance between my parents, even troubled romance, was a significant addendum to the tale of their five-year separation.

Why had my mother recounted for me only the hard times when, in fact, there had been more, and much of it good? If my parents had started out as lovers, then our family wasn't some ragtag "arrangement," and I wasn't just the "reconciliation baby," born to help my mother save her marriage. To learn, even in my 50s, that I'd been born of a love that was, at least in the beginning and for quite a while, no less substantial than many other couples' coup de foudre freed me up, lifted the "curse."

On the other hand, this sweetness in my parents' story also made what eventually happened to them even sadder.

Within a year, everyone in Braddock who had danced at Catherine and Alfredo's wedding knew that the groom had left town for a job and the bride was at home stewing, her weak heart overtaxed as she sat hour after hour at her bedroom window. What cruel control he had over her heart! Perhaps similar to the control America had over him as he prepared the applications to send to the state agencies that would decide if he qualified to sit for the preliminary tests that would determine if he was eligible to apply to take the licensing tests that would permit him, finally, to practice medicine in the U.S. His entire paper trail—each stamped receipt and letter—was still in his file cabinet when he died, as if he was prepared to be asked, at any moment, to account for himself.

As I read the details of my mother's misery, I felt terrible for her, but I didn't see Alfredo as a villain. When he agreed to the marriage, his intentions had been neither malicious nor inappropriately opportunistic—not in his world. If Catherine had not accepted him, there would have been any number of households in Vazzano—or in Calabria, throughout Italy, and in postwar Europe—where daughters and parents would have been happy to sit down and talk marriage with the young doctor. No one in those homes would have been offended by the expectation of a dowry to augment the bride's value. While Catherine eventually felt bought and sold by marriage, I imagine Alfredo felt himself victim of a low-down bait and switch.

In writing workshops, we often talk to students about the importance of developing a *voice on the page*. This is an elusive craft skill, hard to define. And yet there it was, on the pages of my mother's diary. I heard her as her disbelief swelled into outrage. "What I'm about to write isn't anything worth remembering." Often she sounded like an unabashed child standing her ground against a behemoth. There was no way she could win, but I was mesmerized by her efforts to defend her hurt heart.

Her voice held me, and I was also captured by the physical diary— the format of the thing itself. For example, as I read a 1949 entry from their courtship, "At 3:00 we took pictures & he kissed my cheek," my eyes slid down the page to the 1951 entry for that same date: "Dad & Mom argued again & dad again pounding." That visual juxtaposition—

the 1949 romance just a few lines above the 1951 violence—chronicled the year-by-year corrosion of Catherine's innocence in a way I could not ignore. The diary—the object in my hand—told the story of a girl-woman cruelly pressed to her limit.

And yet she held on.

For New Year's in New York, their last honeymoon, Catherine and Alfredo went into the city to see *Il Trovatore*. By now, she, too, loved opera. She stayed in Yonkers a full week. But when Catherine returned to Braddock, she found that her father's fuming was poisoning not only her marriage but also their family life above the bar. As Joe yelled at Stella about their son-in-law, Stella was furious with Joe about the woman friend he had downstairs in the bar. Joe's affair was apparent to everyone, but when confronted, he angrily denied it. One evening in February, he got so upset that he left the apartment and stayed away for two days. Catherine's father was starting to scare her.

She wanted to return to Yonkers, but she caught the flu and was hospitalized. Weeks passed. By the end of April, tension at home was so terrible that Catherine took off for Yonkers, planning to stay with her husband, but when she arrived, Alfredo "didn't seem the same, instead a little cold & we didn't stay half the nite talking as usual."

She sat in the reading chair crammed in next to his cot, staring at her hands—her skinny yellow-gold Italian wedding band—as Alfredo explained that in six weeks his Yonkers internship would end. He'd have to relocate to a new job, he didn't know yet where. His desk was covered with stationery and photostat documents. He'd had to borrow a typewriter from someone and was mailing applications to hospitals all over the country. Of course Alfredo was stressed, but was he really not going to save Catherine from her enraged father?

Reading between Catherine's lines, I could also feel Alfredo's disappointment. Living apart certainly wasn't the marriage he wanted. Months earlier, he'd written in a letter to her, "I need you." But since then, despite their efforts, so many issues of money and her health and logistics had interfered. I'm guessing his heart was broken, too. Now, being practical, Alfredo was telling Catherine that there was no point in renting an apartment in Yonkers for six weeks. Discussion became argument, and in that fury, according to Catherine's diary, Alfredo struck her.

After reading this, I put the diary down. *That didn't happen.* I decided that my mother's use of *struck* felt forced. *She's exaggerating.* Her entry expressed no shock—*maybe because he didn't really hit her?*

You always take his side.

Fully aware of my disloyalty—as a daughter and as a woman—I picked the diary up again, but only because I'd assigned myself the task of reading through to the end.

When she got back to Braddock, Catherine put away her framed wedding photos. In her diary, her husband was no longer "darling." He wasn't even Alfredo. He became Alfred, and over the course of the summer, it occurred to her that she could look into having him deported. She wouldn't see her husband again for four years minus one week. The more immediate marital drama was at home, and the marriage in danger was her mother and father's.

One August Sunday in Braddock, after a family baptism, Catherine and her parents returned to the apartment—everyone was cranky, it was hot—and her parents had an argument that rose and fell and lingered until, in the middle of the night, her father, drunk, roused his wife and daughter, and he turned on Gramma with his fists. His assault was as my mother had described it to me—the hair-pulling—but what she'd never mentioned was that the fight got so bad, cops came to the apartment.

Reading about that night shocked me all over again. Here was the impossible yet inescapable information that at the heart of my grandmother's and mother's stories—at the heart of our family—was domestic violence. To picture an angry hand anywhere near my precious grandmother's face, body, arms, any part of her, was intolerable. Could it be true that at some point in our history we were "that family," the out-of-control neighbors whose agony seeps into the night, gushes so loudly through the windows that someone calls the cops? Or was a patrol car driving by and the shouts so loud that the police parked, shouldered the door open, and ran up unbidden, just in time? What if the cops hadn't shown up?

The Catherine I knew was timorous in the face of any upset: icy roads, flight delays. Her breathing would quicken and her eyes widen, and I'd know she was prepared to notch it up to high panic if someone didn't *do something, quick!* To think of her as a young woman, her mitral valve compromised and her heart broken in love, standing on the sidelines but close enough to hear fists on flesh—

I cover my eyes even now when I think of it, and still, the horror of those moments in August 1951 doesn't go away. I was ready to ignore the entry in which my mother wrote that my father "struck" her, but there was no way I'd ever forget "dad got us out of bed & he bet [sic] mom black & blue."

After that night, Catherine couldn't stay in that angry apartment. For a month, she lived with a family friend. *Who protected Gramma?* And when Catherine returned home, she coped as they all did—by pretending the horror had never happened and praying there'd be no more of it. Stella's brother Jim and the *paesani* probably looked in on her more often, spent extra time down in the bar. It wouldn't help her situation if anyone spoke up, but they kept an eye out. You just had to stay silent about certain things. A few years ago, visiting the cousins my mother grew up with, I mentioned my grandfather's violence, but as close as they had been to my mother and her parents, they knew nothing. "They never told us that stuff."

Even after I learned about Grampa's cruelty to Gramma, I didn't hate him, which surprised me. I was young when I vowed to myself that there were two lapses in a relationship that would immediately make a man dead to me: if he raised a hand or if he cheated. Apparently Grampa was guilty on both counts, but when I read my mother's descriptions of his rage, I felt almost as much pity for him as I felt anger.

Grampa Joe wasn't inclined to tell stories the way Gramma did. But there was one detail my mother told me: As a little boy, he'd had to work as a shepherd, alone in the hills, even during the night. When I heard this, I thought, *How lonely for a kid.*

There's no justification for what he did to Gramma. There are only the facts of his life, which include his loneliness, anger, and inability to cope with whatever untamed beast loped inside him. By nature, Grampa was generous, gentle. When I was a child, he called me "my lily one," which meant *my little one*. It was his role as provider that was challenged when his daughter's marriage went offtrack. Grampa was willing to take Alfredo and Catherine into his home indefinitely. He'd fixed up the newlyweds' bedroom with a new suite of furniture, didn't ask for rent or grocery money—nothing! And yet the young *dottore* wanted more. In front of his fancy new son-in-law, in front of his wife and daughter and their *paesani*, which was the only part of the universe that mattered to them, the bride's father was shamed. And he did not like that. As head of the family, he'd always performed to the best of his ability, and when that wasn't enough, when he had no more to give, he was enraged. I love my grandfather, so I try to understand him, but I can't excuse what he did.

And I can't excuse myself for doubting my mother when she wrote that my father "struck" her, except to say that perhaps both of us, when it came to our fathers, were similarly blind. The patriarchy is buttressed in invisible ways.

When my parents' honeymoons were over and their actual separation began, Catherine pined less, so her diary became easier for me to read. It was a relief to get to the entry in which she wrote about picking up a book she'd put aside months earlier. One Saturday, she listened to *La Traviata* on the radio. Afterward, in one of her longest paragraphs, she drew comparisons between her own life and that of the opera's Violetta, who is ill with consumption and whose love interest is named Alfredo. The next week, Catherine wrote her thoughts about *Rigoletto*. At this point she'd been apart from Alfred for seven months, including four months without a word from him, and she was more fully alive, more available to books, music, ideas, and the world than she'd been since she'd met him. She was 21 now. For better or worse, marriage had matured her.

*

During the winter of 1952, her father's violence resumed. In Catherine's eyes, he was turning into a beast, and in her diary she begged God and the saints to help her and her mother get through this time. It's a sign of Catherine's faith—in her father, as well as in God—that she never doubted this period of horror would pass and their family of three would be restored. But first they had to survive.

I wonder how much of Catherine's decades-long fury at her husband was really the rage she couldn't risk directing at her father. Having seen what it cost her mother to acquiesce, Catherine refused to make *la bella figura*. Keeping a diary of the deep pain that followed her brief joy and passing the story on to me, she stayed loyal to her younger self.

One evening, Catherine's father was so furious, she asked Aunt Mamie to stay overnight, and this was when he pulled out the gun, slammed it down on the kitchen table, and vowed he'd shoot Alfred if he showed up.

Aunt Mamie told him, "Joe, put that away," and eventually he did. Had his wife or daughter said it, he wouldn't have listened to them.

Chapter 21
Joliet

> *For this cause a man shall leave his father and mother, and cleave to his wife.*
> —Mark 10:7

One Sunday afternoon as Catherine sat on a blanket with her cousins at the Kennywood park swimming pool, paging through the newspaper, she came upon an article about a new cardiac procedure: open-heart surgery. After that, in a scrapbook, she collected news write-ups about patients—especially young mothers—who had successfully undergone the surgery. A fair number of patients at that time did not survive. Gramma Stella said no, the surgery was too risky. But Catherine was determined. In February 1953, she had her first open-heart surgery.

"After the operation," Gramma told me, "when they brought me to see her, she was blue, and I thought, *Dear God, my Catherine's dead! What did we do?*"

In early cardiac surgeries, before bypass machines were used to keep blood oxygenated, patients were wrapped in refrigerated blankets to lower the body temperature and halt blood flow temporarily while the heart was operated on. Catherine's color had returned by the time the anesthesia wore off.

In the following months, she resigned herself to a slow convalescence at home. When she was strong enough to take the bus back and forth, she went to secretarial school, preparing herself to stand her ground, with her husband or without him.

*

The next part of Catherine's story, as written in her diary, was different from what she'd told me. On the beach that long-ago Easter, she had led me to believe that in July 1955, Uncle Jim and a few other men—not her father—had accompanied her to Chicago. I pictured an awkward gathering, perhaps outside the hospital where Alfred was working, with Catherine pale and skinny in the shadows. I figured that when the men left, she stayed in Chicago and, to seal the deal, quickly got pregnant. Thus, our family life began, a forced deal between two people who had no choice.

But her diary set me straight. It was April, not July, when Catherine first went to Chicago. The men in the family did drive her there, but she and Alfred spent time alone talking. Mutually they decided that yes, they did want to move forward together.

There really was no other way their situation could have played out. Alfred's mother had made clear he could not return to Italy without his wife. Both Alfred and Catherine had consulted lawyers at various times to inquire about divorce, but they'd each backed off. Bottom line: It wasn't in Alfred's nature to turn his back on a family pledge. He had a rigorous sense of duty. Now, having joined a practice in Joliet, he finally had a salary that could support both him and his wife. During the April visit, he and Catherine decided she would go home to pack her things while he began his job and found an apartment for them.

By the time she returned to Braddock, Alfred was again "darling" on the pages of her diary. I have a photo of Gramma Stella sitting on the couch in her living room, Catherine behind her, on the arm of the couch, both smiling expansively, genuinely. The photo is dated April 1955, right after Catherine's return from reconciling with Alfred. There's so much optimism in Mom's and Gramma's smiles. *Finally, finally.* One year later, posing for more photos, they would sit on that same couch, and between them they'd be holding a baby—me, just a few days old.

July 1955 was a turning point in my parents' story. On the morning of July 9, Catherine boarded the train in Pittsburgh alone, unaccompanied by any of the men who'd previously escorted her, spoken for her, negotiated and battled for her. By ten that evening, she was in Chicago, where Alfred met her at the station.

In her journal entry describing the apartment he'd found—three rooms for eighty dollars a month—Catherine was reserved, writing only that it was "nice," but she was ready to set up housekeeping. Her trunk would arrive in a few days, so on their first morning, she made do with the utensils she found in the kitchen to cook eggs and bacon. The second day, she "redded up" the apartment, as we say in Pittsburgh, and wrote a letter to her parents. She rested and said her prayers. She rinsed out some clothes. Alfred got home from work at six o'clock, and they went out to dinner. Afterward, Catherine set her hair, and before bed, she wrote the last entry in her five-year diary: *Dear out for coffee & he brought me a coffee.* And, with that, their marriage began in earnest.

Chapter 22

I fidanzati

> *Cèrcala ancora, si ti fa piaciri,*
> *oppuru, è miegghju, dàssati cercari.*
> — "A Filicità," Francesco Fazzalari
>
> *Keep looking for it, if that pleases you,*
> *Or, better, let it find you.*
> — "Happiness," Francesco Fazzalari

I'm a mother now myself, so I can imagine the ferocity of Stella's prayers during the days after Catherine's departure to be with Alfred in Joliet. *Dear God. Please. Please.* I see Stella walking the brick sidewalk to St. Michael's church, her head lowered, rosary ring pinched between thumb and forefinger, pocketbook straps hanging in her bent elbow. On a summer Sunday morning, it's likely she crosses paths with a neighbor. By now, Braddock is Stella's home, the streets where she's paced out her adult life. She's 40 years old.

"Hello, missus," the neighbor says.

And Stella smiles, nods, offers a "Yes, hello, missus," but she doesn't interrupt her prayers for chitchat, not this morning. She needs to get to church early, to light candles. What is the best outcome to hope for? That the marriage will last and eventually there will be healthy children. In time, everything she prays for will be realized.

I began reading my mother's diary with resentment and I completed it with gratitude. I was thankful, first, that my guilt lifted when I finally gave her what she'd wanted: I read the narrative of her trauma, beginning to end. In return, she left me information I'd been chasing down most of my life. I needed to learn the layers of my parents' love story, and I also needed to know that my mother and I hadn't been randomly paired; rather, she was essential to me. My native perseverance—a stubbornness that is also steadfastness—had come from her as much as it had from my dad. My mother couldn't save me from pain, but, through her, I acquired a good dose of resilience.

In leaving me her diary, my mother revealed how it had felt to be bundled together with money and goods and offered up as a kid bride. Within her story is also Alfredo's. He, too, was commodified, in a sense purchased by Catherine's nervous parents. What good could come of these transactions that made the heart of anyone—female or male—available as collateral?

Ultimately, my mother's diary freed me up. I learned that *not enough, never enough*—that damning refrain—was an echo from the past, not an accurate self-assessment, not a curse; rather, an epigenetic transmission that tumbled through generations and, I hope, can now peter out. I learned that our unhappiness in marriage was not due to an inherited "legacy" but, rather, began with a series of traceable events—many of them sad, some traumatic—in which trust between people was dismantled and never repaired. *Where to start?*

I'd always known that the intimacy of our family's marriages had been breached, hearts hurt badly, disappointments too raw to heal left to fester. The news in my mother's diary was *how* the patriarchal imperative did its damage to my four most cherished adults, turning those loving people on each other, shaming tenderness, prohibiting independence, collapsing the individual to benefit the group, requiring and rewarding demonstrations of power. In different ways—with rage, violence, abandonment, or by sinking into loneliness, depression, self-denial—each of us said *No! This will not stand! The heart demands more!*

I was proud to be the first in our family born in America, but as a little girl in Braddock, Catherine was the first in her household to go to school beyond fourth grade. She was only 6 when she and her mother landed on the astonishing streets of Braddock, where Catherine served as her mother's translator and interpreter. Maybe I carried our story forward, but my mother was our bridge to the New

World—first as a young daughter and then as a wife. She tried, with everything in her, to fulfill those roles well.

Not all arranged marriages are tragic, I have to remember that. There are places in the world where the quest for *self* does not compete with allegiance to family. There are marriages of convenience in which both parties are equally aware that there is no sentimental tie. And, in many societies, women and men seek their family's assistance in choosing a mate—who holds your interests more fully in their heart than your parents?

Still, I can't deny the struggles I witnessed as a child. That is why I've broken every unwritten rule about family discretion to tell Stella and Joe's, and Catherine and Alfred's stories. I can't let their efforts evaporate and disappear.

These days, when I picture my parents' courtship in Vazzano, a new veil of poignancy falls over the scenes. I see—really *see*—two families trying to survive. One family, needing rescue, reaches for a future in America, while the other family, craving wholeness, reaches back to their original home. They're all gathered around Nonna Anna's long dining table, everyone still a tad overly exuberant and polite as they get used to the idea that two families are becoming one. The war is over but recent enough that one prayer is unanimously offered up: *Ringrazia Dio! Thank God!* To blunt the afternoon sunlight, the slats of the tall wooden shutters are tilted. It is March, but already flies buzz over the after-dinner baskets of cheeses and fruits and whatever else was hauled up from the fields to camouflage the scarcity in Nonna Anna's postwar kitchen. She is trying to re-create, as closely as possible, how things were when Alfredo's father was alive.

Catherine strains to follow the gist of the dinner table conversation while also hyperalert to Alfredo's glances. Will he dare again to tap her sandal under the table with his shoe? Will this be one of the lucky days? Maybe alone for a second in the hallway or in the shadows during the evening walk, they'll have another chance to kiss? Maybe, but these Sunday meals go on for hours. So hard to stay awake. Oh, if only she could slip off her sandals under the table, cool her feet on the tile floor, but her mother's eye is constantly catching Catherine's. Daily, her mother reminds her, *People here are watching you every minute, don't you forget that.*

A ceramic plate of the Last Supper looks down from one wall, and on another hangs a horizontal still life of melons, peaches, limes, and grapes arranged around carcasses of duck, goose, rabbit, and a few birds. It is a garish emblem of bounty, and, sitting below it, the assembled relatives have no inkling that, for all their earnestness, the marriage they are working toward is already spoiling.

The young couple's happiness, even as it begins, is exposed to too many expectations. Each time someone says *America*, the others hear *gold*. Meanwhile, whenever Gramma Stella looks at Catherine, she now thinks *doctor's wife* rather than *invalid*. And when a workingman like Grampa Joe hears *doctor*, of course he's going to think *Has it made in the shade.*

During those formal courtship dinners, no one could have imagined how it would be for a young Italian man to enter a country that still remembered Italy as the enemy. And how would Alfredo launch a career in the U.S. if he was just beginning to learn English? No one could have guessed how low his salary would be during the years before he qualified to sit for medical-licensing tests, to say nothing of how long to complete a residency. Alfredo himself couldn't have imagined it. If the families had considered the practical questions, the wedding most likely never would have happened.

But something about that transatlantic marriage, that alliance of cousins—perhaps just the grand scheme of it—wipes out everyone's native skepticism. So they pour another round of anisette into Nonna Anna's tiny liquor glasses to toast *i fidanzati*.

Saluti!

Across the table, everyone smiles, looking into one another's eyes, or perhaps just above the brow, but eagerly nodding, thinking, *America, doctor, gold*. The pretty misconceptions weave among them like garden snakes coiled in the shade of fig trees blossoming on the parched farm patches from which none of us will ever fully depart.

Epilogue

Inheritance

> *When true simplicity is gained*
> *To bow and to bend*
> *We shall not be ashamed*
> *To turn, turn*
> *Will be our delight*
> *'Till by turning, turning*
> *We come round right*
> —Shaker song by Elder Joseph Brackett

In the height of summer 2013, I am formally concluding my era as *daughter*. Leo and I are in Florida doing the last clean-out of Nonna Catherine and Nonno Alfredo's apartment before putting it on the market. *Keep, or give away, or pitch?* I ask myself this question all day as I empty the curio cabinets and kitchen shelves, drawers and bookshelves.

Yesterday, emptying my mother's desk, I found a journal she kept during the years before my father died, when she was in her early 60s, just a few years older than I am now. Daily, Mom recorded what time she woke and what she cooked for dinner, and these entries summoned up for me the tedium I often felt when we talked on the phone. I was about to toss it, but suddenly, as in the diary of her early marriage, I was reading the news of her heart: "He says stay together for the kids. What a joke."

Shocked, exhaling slowly, I checked the date—just a few years before my dad's death. So, sadly, even at the end, they weren't spared the hard question.

In my mother's TV room, I found a stack of commemorative issues of *People* and *Time* featuring the tragedy of Princess Diana's death. My mother had been a bride so hopeful, she'd modeled her wedding on the future queen's, but eventually she recognized herself in Diana's descent into sorrow.

My parents were both born peasant-poor in the same landlocked village in the toe of Italy; and yet, within one generation, they crossed an ocean and, in time, numerous social strata. Bypassing more than one juncture when they almost parted, they erred and argued, took care of each other and hurt each other, too, but ultimately, their commitment, not their estrangement, won out. The family they created stayed together.

Yesterday, cleaning out my mother's nightstand, I unearthed a box from a jewelry store in Naples, Italy. She'd attached a Post-it: "This is the box from the first gift Dad gave me." Later, among my father's papers, I found the receipt for that gift. The actual bracelet is lost to time, but I couldn't ignore the fact that both my parents held on to evidence of that early offering. For a bride and groom who knew each other so little, it was the exchange of significant gifts that signaled serious intent. Later, in my parents' strained and blessed lifelong marriage, how often did these objects function as a kind of glue, reminding them of family promises and the wish that two strangers with good intentions could join forces and do for their loved ones what needed to be done?

It's your duty, Nonna Anna used to whisper to me. I felt her love and wanted to please her, but it was impossible for me, *americana*, to translate *marriage* into *duty*. How sad that in her time, marriage was, indeed, a tool for a family's survival, as it still is even now in many places in the world.

Today, my grief for my parents' marital sadness is deeper than ever—a purer sadness, because it's finally devoid of guilt. Having learned much of their story, I understand that their marriage was never my task, never mine to save. I feel somber awe for Catherine's and Alfred's arduous singular journeys, which, for better or worse, melded into the journey of their marriage. Released from responsibility, I am spilled onto the wide beach of my own life. What am I meant to accomplish without them?

Keep? Give away? Pitch?

Howard's "you need to separate from your family" was, for years, the goblin under my bed. I misunderstood and hated the concept, and yet I sat with him and others who helped me stare down that ultimate summons—*learn who you are and how to live with yourself*—until it now feels like something that on most days I can manage.

Loneliness is never completely vanquished. The shifting weight of solitude is like those handwoven cloths from Vazzano I use on my bed—sometimes comforting, other times too heavy and oppressive—passed down to me from Gramma Stella.

Earlier today, I spread out my mother's collection of salt and pepper shakers—souvenirs of her travels—along with her china, a flotilla of Lenox swans, and other accoutrements for entertaining. Stacks of coasters. Dozens of shot glasses from Grampa's bar. Does any other household have so many chafing dishes? My parents cherished their friends and relatives, and our family was never more united than when we were preparing for a gathering. Afterward, the good feeling lingered for days, like Mom's delicious leftovers. But sometimes just the four of us shared a spontaneous joy as giddy as any of their well-orchestrated parties. I choose to believe that those times were the truest heart of our family.

Leo asked if we could take Nonno Alfredo's reading chair back to Omaha, where Nonna Catherine's armchair already sits in his room. Like me, Leo surrounds himself with family touchstones. He never met his grandfather but, from my many stories, Leo knows him well enough that yesterday he admonished me, "What would your father say if he knew you let the gas tank get below half-full?"

Tomorrow, a thrift shop team arrives with a pickup truck, and I suspect they'll make a good dent in our inventory. Sometimes I take a break from the clean-out, sit in Dad's chair and stare at the sea, a panorama that reminded us of Calabrian vistas. Much that was meant to happen here *almost* happened, but not quite. My parents hoped that, together with our growing families, my brother and I would fill up their rooms deep into the future. A few of my father's brothers and his two sisters did make it to Florida, but too many visits were about one illness or another, and my father died within four years of moving down here. Our family's Florida was always an "almost place," as my parents' marriage was always *almost* happy, my mother *almost* healthy, all of us *almost* together. But what family anywhere, ever, gets all the time it wishes for or needs?

    It's evening when we finally stop cleaning. Leo has worked hard here, as he has back home. A few weeks ago, he helped me haul Gramma Stella's Hoosier cabinet to an antique shop, where it was purchased by a young chef who'd recently moved to Omaha from New York. He paid almost two hundred dollars, and as a memorial to my grandmother, I donated the money to a local organization that offers shelter to victims of domestic abuse. It's the kind of organization Gramma likely never would have gone to if it had existed in Braddock when she needed help, but I imagine her smiling to know that "those old sticks of furniture" from her Braddock kitchen are doing some good for women in Omaha today.

    There's still light in the sky as Leo and I make our way through the big-leafed palm trees to the pool. In summer, there are so few people around, it's all ours. The sun is lowering, and the surface of the water is covered with the reflection of fronds, featherlike, something you could use to tickle a child. We dive in, swim a few laps, and then Leo and I stand in the shallow end and toss a ball back and forth, back and forth to each other. I revel in this game because it allows me to keep my gaze on his face. When he misses, he dives into the intricately patterned water and comes up smiling. Turquoise pool, amber light swaddling my son, our evening another episode in the golden mystery of family life. I lower my face into the privacy of the water and thank my parents for this inheritance.

THE END

Afterword

A great memoir is one that is truthful. It can be a glorious opera coat or a suit of armor, depending upon the writer and her ability to align the reader, from her perch, with her point of view of the world. Anna Monardo's story is both silk and steel, a garment of beauty and also of protection. Her family story is one of strength and vulnerability, the two chambers of the immigrant heart. Her Italian roots were fed and watered by women who served their husbands and sons and taught their daughters to do the same. If this seems old-fashioned, look around. We're still at it.

From the moment Anna tries on her mother's wedding gown, through a career in the erudite world of books and magazines, to the publication of her heralded debut novel, through the process of becoming an educator, and, after much determination, a mother herself, *After Italy* is, in fact, the story of the coat Anna built and wears to this day. The garment's buttons strain from movement and age, held together at once by a need to understand and a need to grow from the experiences of her childhood, but it still fits.

The saga of this memoir began with a curious young girl who spent hours poring over her parents' wedding album, a 1950s-era storybook with her mother in that gown on the arm of her smiling father. As Anna flipped the pages, she was in heaven. That cake! The cars! The cousins! Like her mother, Stella, before her, Anna's mother, Caterina (Catherine), marries quickly, almost like a roll of the dice, that fast, fingers crossed, hopeful to hit the jackpot. Their choices become Anna's work on the page. The author's wanderlust and impatience with romantic love, like her gramma's, like her mother's, is inborn, it seems. Anna writes of their marriages with a view from the table leg of *la tavola*, the center of the Italian home. That particular point of view informs this memoir at every turn. Anna Monardo, unlike her mother and grandmother, is always looking up, even when she too experiences inevitable heartbreak.

Ribboned through this gorgeously rendered true story, the professor Anna Monardo emerges. Her cultural touchstones are spot on. The novella *The Light in the Piazza* and others are influences, but more importantly, they encourage Anna to look at her family life in a cultural context. It isn't hard to find Italian Americans with roots in the heel of the boot that she can call upon to feel connection, but she also finds simpatico souls in the world around her. The poverty that brought her family from Vazzano (her family's village) to America becomes the runway of this memoir but not the ride.

The flat fields of Nebraska are like empty sheets of paper, which Anna Monardo filled with her family history and the secrets she finally felt free enough to share. The storytelling in *After Italy* is restless and evocative. Anna comes to understand her working-class family because she shares their determination and stamina, but of course all of it is fragile, like that wedding gown. There are broken hearts along the way. Failed romances. Threats of divorce. Separation. Widowhood. Modern problems appear in the book, not as cracks and fissures in the old stone wall, but as the wall itself. Anna Monardo shares it all with the reader and, by example, encourages us not to give up—and that means on the wily, strange, unpredictable, joyous, and painful past. Hold on to it. Savor it. It's the treasure. She knows.

Adriana Trigiani
NEW YORK CITY
JULY 15, 2020

Acknowledgments

What excellent company I've had during the years I worked on this book, and what exceptional support, starting with Gail Hochman, remarkable agent and treasured friend.

Fred Gardaphé, Anthony Tamburri, and Paolo Giordano, thank you for believing in *After Italy* and giving the book a home at Bordighera Press. To Nicholas Grosso, managing editor supreme, so much gratitude.

Lanny De Vuono, Susan Aizenberg, and Meghan Daum, you were indefatigable in your willingness to enter this story with me, draft after draft after draft. You buoyed me until finally it happened: a book. My love to you, and my thanks.

Adriana Trigiani, your generous spirit is legendary. Thank you for bringing your wise eye to this story and for your thoughtful reflection on "the two chambers of the immigrant heart"—I love your phrase. It's an honor to round out this narrative with your Afterword, which provides beautiful context for the reader.

Cathleen Medwick, you were a dream editor for the two excerpts that appeared in *More*, editing with a light hand and, with a few insightful questions, quickly getting to the heart of each piece. Just as deftly, you helped me untangle the full manuscript when it was trying to do too many things at once. Thank you.

For sharing your vast expertise during various stages of this project, many thanks to Joanne Camas, Mary Coady-Leeper, Caroline Coppel, Lynn Anderson De Mott, Hattie Fletcher, Lee Gutkind, Anne Horowitz, Kristen Luther, Connie J. Mableson, and Cheryl Murray.

I am grateful to the editors of the publications where excerpts of this memoir first appeared: *Cimarron Review, Creative Nonfiction,*

Exquisite Pandemic, Fourth Genre and the anthology *Five Years of Fourth Genre, Hotel Amerika, More,* and *Ovunque Siamo.*

My work on this book was helped greatly by residencies at Yaddo and the Kimmel Harding Nelson Center for the Arts, as well as by grants from the University of Nebraska at Omaha and the Nebraska Arts Council. For these invaluable forms of support, my deepest thanks.

What a lucky teacher I am to have had a home for twenty-seven years in the Writer's Workshop, the BFA creative-writing program at the University of Nebraska at Omaha. I'm profoundly grateful to the students, colleagues, and visiting writers I've had the great pleasure to work with in magical Room 218—especially Teresa Carmody, Kevin Clouther, Lisa Fay Coutley, Todd Robinson, Lisa Sandlin, Miles Waggener, and Ken White. Thanks also to our colleagues and students throughout UNO's exceptional School of the Arts.

There are many friends and colleagues I'm indebted to for your support as this book evolved. You offered to read the manuscript and encouraged me to continue when I had doubts, you listened as I talked through the story, and you generously shared your own family stories. You graciously invited me into your homes and offered me quiet rooms to work in; you joined me for long walks, long talks, long Zoom visits, long meals, long digressions, and quick responses when, now and then, something felt urgent. My deepest appreciation to Jean Alexander and Lance Duncan, Steve Carter, Barbara Collier, Patricia Henley, the Holyoke crowd, the Jackson Street crowd, Debbie Jewell, Tyler Kelley, Marla Kinney, Antoinette and Marty Marra, Bosa Raditsa, Linda Rossi, Sue William Silverman, Ivan Solotaroff, Nance Van Winckel, and Max Westler. Maria Teresa Maenza-Vanderboegh, Sara Marzioli, and Giusy Sciacca, you brought Italy to Omaha. *Mille grazie!* Thanks to my friends in two different book groups—one on Zoom, one in person, both beloved.

The following books were invaluable as I worked on this project: *Dialogue with Erik Erikson* by Richard I. Evans; *u Vizzarru: Cronaca Calabrese* and *Paisi e Città: Versi Dialettali Calabresi* by Francesco Fazzalari; *Epigenetics: The Ultimate Mystery of Inheritance* by Richard C. Francis; *Da Subsicinum a Vazzano* by Sharo Gambino; *Naples '44* by Norman Lewis; *Making Democracy Work: Civic Traditions in Modern*

Italy by Robert D. Putnam; and *Benevolence and Betrayal: Five Italian Jewish Families Under Fascism* by Alexander Stille.

At the heart of *After Italy* is my family—my beloved deceased parents, grandparents, *zie* and *zii*, who are often with me in my writing room; and, of course, the ever-dependable net of my spectacular *zie*, nieces, nephews, and two generations of cousins and in-laws. Most of us are descendants of those brave souls who left Vazzano and nearby villages and headed to Braddock, Toronto, and various other parts of North America, Italy, Australia, and South America. They left with us in mind, determined to build a better future. At this point, we're a stretched-out string of *cugini* and *paesani*, but we grew up together, as our parents grew up together, so you are always in my heart.

As for my son, Leo, and my brother, Paul: You two are the best.

About the Author

ANNA MONARDO grew up in Pittsburgh, with strong ties to her Calabrian family. Her first novel, *The Courtyard of Dreams* (Doubleday), set largely in southern Italy, was translated into German, Norwegian, and Danish; featured in the Selected Shorts reading series at Symphony Space in New York City; and nominated for a PEN/Hemingway Award and recommended for the National Book Critics Circle Awards. Excerpts from her second novel, *Falling In Love with Natassia* (Doubleday), first appeared in *Prairie Schooner* and were nominated for Pushcart Prizes; one excerpt was awarded *Prairie Schooner*'s Hugh J. Luke Award for Short Fiction. Her work has been anthologized in *The Dream Book Anthology of Writing by Italian-American Women*, *Five Years of Fourth Genre*, and *A Different Plain: Contemporary Nebraska Fiction Writers*. Excerpts from *After Italy: A Family Memoir of Arranged Marriage* were published in *Cimarron Review*, *Creative Nonfiction*, *Exquisite Pandemic*, *Fourth Genre*, *Hotel Amerika*, *More*, and *Ovunque Siamo*. Monardo's fiction, poetry, and essays have appeared in *The Sun*, *Birmingham Poetry Review*, *HuffPost*, *Indiana Review*, *Poets & Writers*, and other magazines and journals. A recipient of fellowships from Yaddo, the Djerassi Foundation, and the Virginia Center for the Creative Arts, as well as three fellowships from the Nebraska Arts Council, she teaches in the Writer's Workshop at the University of Nebraska at Omaha. Visit annamonardo.com

VIA Folios
A refereed book series dedicated to the culture of Italians and Italian Americans.

JOEY NICOLETTI. *Extinction Wednesday*. Vol. 168. Poetry.
MARIA FAMÀ. *Trigger*. Vol. 167. Poetry.
WILLI Q MINN. *What? Nothing*. Vol. 166. Poetry.
RICHARD VETERE. *She's Not There*. Vol. 165. Literature.
FRANK GIOIA. *Mercury Man*. Vol. 164. Literature.
LUISA M. GIULIANETTI. *Agrodolce*. Vol. 163. Literature.
ANGELO ZEOLLA. *The Bronx Unbound ovvero i versi bronxesi*. Vol. 162. Poetry.
NICHOLAS A. DiCHARIO. *Giovanni's Tree*. Vol. 161. Literature.
ADELE ANNESI. *What She Takes Away*. Vol. 160. Novel.
ANNIE RACHELE LANZILLOTTO. *Whaddyacall the Wind?*. Vol. 159. Memoir.
JULIA LISELLA. *Our Lively Kingdom*. Vol. 158. Poetry.
MARK CIABATTARI. *When the Mask Slips*. Vol. 157. Novel.
JENNIFER MARTELLI. *The Queen of Queens*. Vol. 156. Poetry.
TONY TADDEI. *The Sons of the Santorelli*. Vol. 155. Literature.
FRANCO RICCI. *Preston Street • Corso Italias*. Vol. 154. History.
MIKE FIORITO. *The Hated Ones*. Vol. 153. Literature.
PATRICIA DUNN. *Last Stop on the 6*. Vol. 152. Novel.
WILLIAM BOELHOWER. *Immigrant Autobiography*. Vol. 151. Literary Criticism.
MARC DIPAOLO. *Fake Italian*. Vol. 150. Literature.
GAIL REITANO. *Italian Love Cake*. Vol. 149. Novel.
VINCENT PANELLA. *Sicilian Dreams*. Vol. 148. Novel.
MARK CIABATTARI. *The Literal Truth: Rizzoli Dreams of Eating the Apple of Earthly Delights*. Vol. 147. Novel.
MARK CIABATTARI. *Dreams of An Imaginary New Yorker Named Rizzoli*. Vol. 146. Novel.
LAURETTE FOLK. *The End of Aphrodite*. Vol. 145. Novel.
ANNA CITRINO. *A Space Between*. Vol. 144. Poetry
MARIA FAMÀ. *The Good for the Good*. Vol. 143. Poetry.
ROSEMARY CAPPELLO. *Wonderful Disaster*. Vol. 142. Poetry.
B. AMORE. *Journeys on the Wheel*. Vol. 141. Poetry.
ALDO PALAZZESCHI. *The Manifestos of Aldo Palazzeschi*. Vol 140. Literature.
ROSS TALARICO. *The Reckoning*. Vol 139. Poetry.
MICHELLE REALE. *Season of Subtraction*. Vol 138. Poetry.
MARISA FRASCA. *Wild Fennel*. Vol 137. Poetry.
RITA ESPOSITO WATSON. *Italian Kisses*. Vol. 136. Memoir.
SARA FRUNER. *Bitter Bites from Sugar Hills*. Vol. 135. Poetry.
KATHY CURTO. *Not for Nothing*. Vol. 134. Memoir.
JENNIFER MARTELLI. *My Tarantella*. Vol. 133. Poetry.
MARIA TERRONE. *At Home in the New World*. Vol. 132. Essays.
GIL FAGIANI. *Missing Madonnas*. Vol. 131. Poetry.
LEWIS TURCO. *The Sonnetarium*. Vol. 130. Poetry.
JOE AMATO. *Samuel Taylor's Hollywood Adventure*. Vol. 129. Novel.

BEA TUSIANI. *Con Amore*. Vol. 128. Memoir.
MARIA GIURA. *What My Father Taught Me*. Vol. 127. Poetry.
STANISLAO PUGLIESE. *A Century of Sinatra*. Vol. 126. Popular Culture.
TONY ARDIZZONE. *The Arab's Ox*. Vol. 125. Novel.
PHYLLIS CAPELLO. *Packs Small Plays Big*. Vol. 124. Literature.
FRED GARDAPHÉ. *Read 'em and Reap*. Vol. 123. Criticism.
JOSEPH A. AMATO. *Diagnostics*. Vol 122. Literature.
DENNIS BARONE. *Second Thoughts*. Vol 121. Poetry.
OLIVIA K. CERRONE. *The Hunger Saint*. Vol 120. Novella.
GARIBLADI M. LAPOLLA. *Miss Rollins in Love*. Vol 119. Novel.
JOSEPH TUSIANI. *A Clarion Call*. Vol 118. Poetry.
JOSEPH A. AMATO. *My Three Sicilies*. Vol 117. Poetry & Prose.
MARGHERITA COSTA. *Voice of a Virtuosa and Coutesan*. Vol 116. Poetry.
NICOLE SANTALUCIA. *Because I Did Not Die*. Vol 115. Poetry.
MARK CIABATTARI. *Preludes to History*. Vol 114. Poetry.
HELEN BAROLINI. *Visits*. Vol 113. Novel.
ERNESTO LIVORNI. *The Fathers' America*. Vol 112. Poetry.
MARIO B. MIGNONE. *The Story of My People*. Vol 111. Non-fiction.
GEORGE GUIDA. *The Sleeping Gulf*. Vol 110. Poetry.
JOEY NICOLETTI. *Reverse Graffiti*. Vol 109. Poetry.
GIOSE RIMANELLI. *Il mestiere del furbo*. Vol 108. Criticism.
LEWIS TURCO. *The Hero Enkidu*. Vol 107. Poetry.
AL TACCONELLI. *Perhaps Fly*. Vol 106. Poetry.
RACHEL GUIDO DEVRIES. *A Woman Unknown in Her Bones*. Vol 105. Poetry.
BERNARD BRUNO. *A Tear and a Tear in My Heart*. Vol 104. Non-fiction.
FELIX STEFANILE. *Songs of the Sparrow*. Vol 103. Poetry.
FRANK POLIZZI. *A New Life with Bianca*. Vol 102. Poetry.
GIL FAGIANI. *Stone Walls*. Vol 101. Poetry.
LOUISE DESALVO. *Casting Off*. Vol 100. Fiction.
MARY JO BONA. *I Stop Waiting for You*. Vol 99. Poetry.
RACHEL GUIDO DEVRIES. *Stati zitt, Josie*. Vol 98. Children's Literature. $8
GRACE CAVALIERI. *The Mandate of Heaven*. Vol 97. Poetry.
MARISA FRASCA. *Via incanto*. Vol 96. Poetry.
DOUGLAS GLADSTONE. *Carving a Niche for Himself*. Vol 95. History.
MARIA TERRONE. *Eye to Eye*. Vol 94. Poetry.
CONSTANCE SANCETTA. *Here in Cerchio*. Vol 93. Local History.
MARIA MAZZIOTTI GILLAN. *Ancestors' Song*. Vol 92. Poetry.
MICHAEL PARENTI. *Waiting for Yesterday: Pages from a Street Kid's Life*. Vol 90. Memoir.
ANNIE LANZILLOTTO. *Schistsong*. Vol 89. Poetry.
EMANUEL DI PASQUALE. *Love Lines*. Vol 88. Poetry.
CAROSONE & LOGIUDICE. *Our Naked Lives*. Vol 87. Essays.
JAMES PERICONI. *Strangers in a Strange Land: A Survey of Italian-Language American Books*. Vol 86. Book History.
DANIELA GIOSEFFI. *Escaping La Vita Della Cucina*. Vol 85. Essays.
MARIA FAMÀ. *Mystics in the Family*. Vol 84. Poetry.

ROSSANA DEL ZIO. *From Bread and Tomatoes to Zuppa di Pesce "Ciambotto".* Vol. 83. Memoir.
LORENZO DELBOCA. *Polentoni.* Vol 82. Italian Studies.
SAMUEL GHELLI. *A Reference Grammar.* Vol 81. Italian Language.
ROSS TALARICO. *Sled Run.* Vol 80. Fiction.
FRED MISURELLA. *Only Sons.* Vol 79. Fiction.
FRANK LENTRICCHIA. *The Portable Lentricchia.* Vol 78. Fiction.
RICHARD VETERE. *The Other Colors in a Snow Storm.* Vol 77. Poetry.
GARIBALDI LAPOLLA. *Fire in the Flesh.* Vol 76 Fiction & Criticism.
GEORGE GUIDA. *The Pope Stories.* Vol 75 Prose.
ROBERT VISCUSI. *Ellis Island.* Vol 74. Poetry.
ELENA GIANINI BELOTTI. *The Bitter Taste of Strangers Bread.* Vol 73. Fiction.
PINO APRILE. *Terroni.* Vol 72. Italian Studies.
EMANUEL DI PASQUALE. *Harvest.* Vol 71. Poetry.
ROBERT ZWEIG. *Return to Naples.* Vol 70. Memoir.
AIROS & CAPPELLI. *Guido.* Vol. 69. Italian/American Studies.
FRED GARDAPHÉ. *Moustache Pete is Dead! Long Live Moustache Pete!.* Vol. 67. Literature/Oral History.
PAOLO RUFFILLI. *Dark Room/Camera oscura.* Vol 66. Poetry.
HELEN BAROLINI. *Crossing the Alps.* Vol 65. Fiction.
COSMO FERRARA. *Profiles of Italian Americans.* Vol 64. Italian Americana.
GIL FAGIANI. *Chianti in Connecticut.* Vol 63. Poetry.
BASSETTI & D'ACQUINO. *Italic Lessons.* Vol 62. Italian/American Studies.
CAVALIERI & PASCARELLI, Eds. *The Poet's Cookbook.* Vol 61. Poetry/Recipes.
EMANUEL DI PASQUALE. *Siciliana.* Vol 60. Poetry.
NATALIA COSTA, Ed. *Bufalini.* Vol 59. Poetry.
RICHARD VETERE. *Baroque.* Vol 58. Fiction.
LEWIS TURCO. *La Famiglia/The Family.* Vol 57. Memoir.
NICK JAMES MILETI. *The Unscrupulous.* Vol 56. Humanities.
BASSETTI. ACCOLLA. D'AQUINO. *Italici: An Encounter with Piero Bassetti.* Vol 55. Italian Studies.
GIOSE RIMANELLI. *The Three-legged One.* Vol 54. Fiction.
CHARLES KLOPP. *Bele Antiche Stòrie.* Vol 53. Criticism.
JOSEPH RICAPITO. *Second Wave.* Vol 52. Poetry.
GARY MORMINO. *Italians in Florida.* Vol 51. History.
GIANFRANCO ANGELUCCI. *Federico F.* Vol 50. Fiction.
ANTHONY VALERIO. *The Little Sailor.* Vol 49. Memoir.
ROSS TALARICO. *The Reptilian Interludes.* Vol. 48. Poetry.
RACHEL GUIDO DE VRIES. *Teeny Tiny Tino's Fishing Story.* Vol 47. Children's Literature.
EMANUEL DI PASQUALE. *Writing Anew.* Vol 46. Poetry.
MARIA FAMÀ. *Looking For Cover.* Vol 45. Poetry.
ANTHONY VALERIO. *Toni Cade Bambara's One Sicilian Night.* Vol 44. Poetry.
EMANUEL CARNEVALI. *Furnished Rooms.* Vol 43. Poetry.
BRENT ADKINS. et al., Ed. *Shifting Borders. Negotiating Places.* Vol 42. Conference.

GEORGE GUIDA. *Low Italian*. Vol 41. Poetry.
GARDAPHÈ, GIORDANO, TAMBURRI. *Introducing Italian Americana*. Vol 40. Italian/American Studies.
DANIELA GIOSEFFI. *Blood Autumn/Autunno di sangue*. Vol 39. Poetry.
FRED MISURELLA. *Lies to Live By*. Vol 38. Stories.
STEVEN BELLUSCIO. *Constructing a Bibliography*. Vol 37. Italian Americana.
ANTHONY JULIAN TAMBURRI, Ed. *Italian Cultural Studies 2002*. Vol 36. Essays.
BEA TUSIANI. *con amore*. Vol 35. Memoir.
FLAVIA BRIZIO-SKOV, Ed. *Reconstructing Societies in the Aftermath of War*. Vol 34. History.
TAMBURRI. et al., Eds. *Italian Cultural Studies 2001*. Vol 33. Essays.
ELIZABETH G. MESSINA, Ed. *In Our Own Voices*. Vol 32. Italian/American Studies.
STANISLAO G. PUGLIESE. *Desperate Inscriptions*. Vol 31. History.
HOSTERT & TAMBURRI, Eds. *Screening Ethnicity*. Vol 30. Italian/American Culture.
G. PARATI & B. LAWTON, Eds. *Italian Cultural Studies*. Vol 29. Essays.
HELEN BAROLINI. *More Italian Hours*. Vol 28. Fiction.
FRANCO NASI, Ed. *Intorno alla Via Emilia*. Vol 27. Culture.
ARTHUR L. CLEMENTS. *The Book of Madness & Love*. Vol 26. Poetry.
JOHN CASEY, et al. *Imagining Humanity*. Vol 25. Interdisciplinary Studies.
ROBERT LIMA. *Sardinia/Sardegna*. Vol 24. Poetry.
DANIELA GIOSEFFI. *Going On*. Vol 23. Poetry.
ROSS TALARICO. *The Journey Home*. Vol 22. Poetry.
EMANUEL DI PASQUALE. *The Silver Lake Love Poems*. Vol 21. Poetry.
JOSEPH TUSIANI. *Ethnicity*. Vol 20. Poetry.
JENNIFER LAGIER. *Second Class Citizen*. Vol 19. Poetry.
FELIX STEFANILE. *The Country of Absence*. Vol 18. Poetry.
PHILIP CANNISTRARO. *Blackshirts*. Vol 17. History.
LUIGI RUSTICHELLI, Ed. *Seminario sul racconto*. Vol 16. Narrative.
LEWIS TURCO. *Shaking the Family Tree*. Vol 15. Memoirs.
LUIGI RUSTICHELLI, Ed. *Seminario sulla drammaturgia*. Vol 14. Theater/Essays.
FRED GARDAPHÈ. *Moustache Pete is Dead! Long Live Moustache Pete!*. Vol 13. Oral Literature.
JONE GAILLARD CORSI. *Il libretto d'autore. 1860 - 1930*. Vol 12. Criticism.
HELEN BAROLINI. *Chiaroscuro: Essays of Identity*. Vol 11. Essays.
PICARAZZI & FEINSTEIN, Eds. *An African Harlequin in Milan*. Vol 10. Theater/Essays.
JOSEPH RICAPITO. *Florentine Streets & Other Poems*. Vol 9. Poetry.
FRED MISURELLA. *Short Time*. Vol 8. Novella.
NED CONDINI. *Quartettsatz*. Vol 7. Poetry.
ANTHONY JULIAN TAMBURRI, Ed. *Fuori: Essays by Italian/American Lesbiansand Gays*. Vol 6. Essays.

ANTONIO GRAMSCI. P. Verdicchio. Trans. & Intro. *The Southern Question.*
Vol 5. Social Criticism.
DANIELA GIOSEFFI. *Word Wounds & Water Flowers.* Vol 4. Poetry. $8
WILEY FEINSTEIN. *Humility's Deceit: Calvino Reading Ariosto Reading Calvino.*
Vol 3. Criticism.
PAOLO A. GIORDANO, Ed. *Joseph Tusiani: Poet. Translator. Humanist.*
Vol 2. Criticism.
ROBERT VISCUSI. *Oration Upon the Most Recent Death of Christopher Columbus.*
Vol 1. Poetry.

www.ingramcontent.com/pod-product-compliance
Lightning Source LLC
Chambersburg PA
CBHW031436160426
43195CB00010BB/747